TRAILBLAZING
BLACK
WOMEN
of
WASHINGTON STATE

MARILYN MORGAN

THE
History
PRESS

Published by The History Press
Charleston, SC
www.historypress.com

First published 2022

Manufactured in the United States

ISBN 9781467150422

Library of Congress Control Number: 2022935430

This book is dedicated to all women—those who came before us, those currently are with us and those who have yet to come. May we learn from them, walk with them and teach them. May we continue to learn and prosper.

CONTENTS

PREFACE

When I was a student, I rarely studied Black women's contributions to America. When I saw the movie *Hidden Figures*, it made me think about the "hidden figures" of Black women who have been and still are essential parts of the development of American society. From the women's suffrage movement to civil rights, medicine and the legislature, Black women have broken barriers and made life-changing contributions.

After the Civil War, many Black Americans hoped for a new beginning, eager to explore their newfound freedom. Black women hoped for that freedom also.

Civil rights icon Julian Bond said it best when he described the strengths that women brought to the table in an Associated Press interview in 2005. "History has a saying: 'Women hold up half the world.' In the case of the civil rights movement, it is probably three-quarters of the world."

In this book, I want to highlight the many contributions that the Black women of Washington State have contributed to the state and the world.

Women like Susie Revels Cayton. She moved to Seattle in 1896 to marry her fiancé, Harold Cayton. When women, particularly Black women, had no voice and lacked education, she had both. She was an activist and newspaper editor who advocated for equal rights and education for women. She was likely the first Black woman who had an article published by the *Seattle Post-Intelligencer* (*Seattle P-I*).

Letitia Graves established the first Seattle chapter of the NAACP in 1913 and was the chapter's first president.

Young future suffragists on a float at a citywide festival in July 1911. *Photograph courtesy of the Museum of History and Industry, photography collection.*

Professor Alice Ball was a chemist who discovered the "Ball Method," the most effective treatment for leprosy during the early twentieth century.

Joyce Dewitty broke the color barrier by becoming the first Black teacher hired by the Seattle Public School System.

Rosa Franklin was the first Black woman to serve as a state senator in 1990.

Black women continue to influence and prosper in Washington, contributing and impacting the lives of people who live in the state of Washington and beyond. This book is in no way inclusive of all the great Black women pioneers in Washington—there are many more.

ACKNOWLEDGEMENTS

I want to thank all of the people and organizations whose help was instrumental in bringing this book to fruition.

Anita Warmflash (Boeing Rosie the Riveter Series)
Anna Elam (MOHAI)
BlackPast.com
Cynthia Tucker, historian of the Washington State Federation of Colored Women's Clubs
Eric Bronson
Esther Mumford (Bicentennial Oral History Program)
Everett Historic Theater
Everett Public Library
Fabienne Brooks
HistoryLink.org
Professor James Gregory (Seattle Civil Rights and Labor History Project)
Jeff Jewell (Whatcom Museum)
Jesse Koon (Tacoma Historical Society)
John Hughes (Washington State Legacy Project)
Karen Fargas (The Living Arts Cultural Heritage Project, Kitsap County)
Kitsap Historical Museum
Lee Pierce, Washington secretary of state
Library of Congress
Lisa Labovitch, historian of the Everett Public Library

Dr. Maxine Mimms
Meaghan Kahlo (Seattle Public Schools)
Museum of History and Industry Seattle (MOHAI)
National Archives
Phyllis Wheatley (YWCA)
Robin Fiorillo (Spokane Schools)
Rosalee Lander, consultant
Seattle Civil Rights and Labor History Project
Seattle Municipal Archives Photography Collection
Seattle Public Library (Central and Greenwood Branches)
Seattle Public Schools Archives
Steve Wallace
Tacoma History Museum
Trevor Griffey (Seattle Civil Rights and Labor History Project)
Washington State Archives
Washington State Digital Archives (Bicentennial Oral History Program, Black Project 1975–1976)
Washington State Historical Society
Washington State Legacy Project
Washington State Library
Whitworth College

1

SUSIE REVELS CAYTON

Writer, Activist and Newspaper Editor

Susie Revels Cayton was a third-generation free Black woman. She was a college graduate, an activist for women and children, a clubwoman and the first Black woman to become a newspaper editor.

Susie Revels Cayton was an unusual Black woman for her time. She was an educated woman who worked in journalism, including as a newspaper editor, making her the first Black woman in that position and presumably the first woman editor in Seattle. She was an advocate for Black Americans' advancement and was a third-generation free Black American.

She was born in 1870 in Mississippi. She moved to Seattle in 1896 to join her soon-to-be husband, Horace Cayton. They were one of the earliest Black couples to move to the new Seattle Territory, bolstering their place as one of the most prominent Black families and activists in Washington. The Caytons' legacy remains today.

It is not a surprise that Revels Cayton was politically active and involved in civil rights. Her father was Hiram Rhodes Revels, a Republican and the first Black American elected senator to serve in the U.S. Congress. Her mother was Phoebe Bass Revels, a Quaker from Zanesville, Ohio. Revels was elected to the Senate in 1870, during the Reconstruction era after the Civil War. The Emancipation Proclamation granted enslaved people their freedom. The era afforded former enslaved people, among other things, the right to vote and the right to hold political office. The Reconstruction era lasted from 1865 to 1877 and attempted to heal a divided country and remedy racial inequality.

Left: Susie Revels Cayton was the first Black woman editor of a newspaper. *Public domain*.

Right: Horace Cayton Sr. was the son of an enslaved person but rose to become a newspaper publisher and the owner of the longest-running Black-owned paper (*Seattle Republican*) in Washington State. It was published from 1894 to 1913. *Public domain*.

Revels Cayton's father, Hiram Revels, was born in North Carolina on September 27, 1827. He was born free, as was his father. Revels's accomplishments were vast. He studied theology and became a minister of the African Methodist Church. After the Civil War, he moved to Natchez, Mississippi, where he lived with his wife and five children. In 1869, he won the election to the state senate. In 1870, Revels received an appointment as the Republican senator for Mississippi the same year his daughter Susie was born. After serving one term in the senate, he returned to Mississippi and became president of Alcorn State University and Mechanical College (now Alcorn State University).

Susie Revels Cayton had a privileged life, vastly different from most Black Americans at the time. She was brilliant, and at sixteen years old, she earned her degree from State Normal School (now Rust University, a historically Black college) in Holly Springs, Mississippi. Revels Cayton taught school for three years. She returned to college and received another degree in nursing, all by the time she was twenty-three years old.

Hiram Revels was Susie Revels Cayton's father and was the first Black man elected to the U.S. Congress after the Civil War. *Photograph courtesy of the Library of Congress, 2017894095.*

While visiting Mississippi, Revels met her husband, Horace R. Cayton, a political activist and newspaper publisher. After working for other newspapers in Seattle, including the *Seattle P-I*, he decided to publish his own newspaper, the *Seattle Republican*. While living in Mississippi, she began reading the *Seattle Republican*, sent to her father by Horace Cayton. He was a student at Alcorn University when Revels's father headed the university. She loved the art of writing and was a writer in her own right. She was impressed by the paper. Revels Cayton started submitting articles and short stories while also corresponding with Horace Cayton. The first article she had published by the *Seattle Republican* was titled "Negroes at the Atlanta Exposition." Horace Cayton was impressed with her writing style, content and Revel herself.

Cayton decided to launch his own paper and named it the *Seattle Republican*. The *Seattle Republican* was launched in 1894 and went out of business in 1913, making it the longest-running and largest Black-owned newspaper in the United States. The two embarked on a long-distance romance.

Cayton was born in 1859 as an enslaved person. His father was enslaved, and his mother was the plantation owner's white daughter. Cayton graduated from Alcorn State in Mississippi.

Revels Cayton moved to Seattle six months after that article was published in 1896. She and Horace were married on July 12, 1896. They started a family of five children: Ruth, Madge, Lillie, Horace Jr. and Revels. They also

The Cayton family on their front porch, circa 1904. *From left to right*: Ruth (*blurred*), Emma (niece), Susie (*holding Horace Jr.*), Horace and Madge (*seated*). *Photograph courtesy of the Seattle Archives.*

raised a niece, Emma, after her mother died and their granddaughter Susan after their daughter Ruth died.

Revels Cayton was excited to write for her husband's paper. The paper's mission was to present Black people positively and appeal to a multiracial readership. But its writers found out it was no easy task to satisfy everyone.

The Seattle Civil Rights and History Project's website cites this quote from the *Seattle Republican* (1906): "A colored subscriber wants the paper stopped because it has nothing in it. A white subscriber orders his paper discontinued because 'It has too much colored news in it.' So, between the two, the financier has the devil's own time to keep things going."

Today, the Caytons would be known as a power couple. Revels Cayton became the associate editor of the *Seattle Republican*. The weekly edition was sold for a nickel a copy, and a year's subscription cost two dollars; the paper was very successful during its run.

Revels Cayton was an advocate for women's equality. Her articles and editorials often addressed the importance of education for women. One of her editorials supporting education for women stated: "Should women receive classical education has been asked by some. There can be but one answer to this question, and that is yes. Water cannot rise higher than its level, and so is it with the human family. The mental development of any person is dependent almost solely on the woman's efforts. It is the hand that rocks the cradle that also directs the destinies of the human family."

The *Seattle Republican* was known across the country because Seattle was a port city where visitors and tourists would take the newspaper to different cities. According to the Seattle Civil Rights and Labor History's website, the Caytons were known countrywide. They often entertained such famous visitors as renowned poet Langston Hughes and educator Booker T. Washington, which is not surprising since Revels Cayton was also a woman of culture. She hosted lavish dinner parties for her famous guests, many music recitals and plays at her home.

Revels Cayton worried about the self-esteem of Black children. In an article titled "Black Baby Dolls," she warned Black parents of the psychological harm done if Black children only played with white dolls. She encouraged Black parents to seek out Black dolls for their children, urging them to make their own dolls if retail stores refused to sell Black dolls. That was forward thinking for her time—maybe even prophetic. Years later, in 1939, Dr. Kenneth Clark and his wife, Mamie, conducted a psychological experiment with Black children using dolls. The psychologists used the experiment to show how stereotypes and racism can be internalized and ingrained in children, resulting in self-loathing or self-hate. The children were given Black dolls and white dolls to play with and asked a series of questions. The children ascribed positive traits to the white dolls, saying they were pretty and nice. Inversely, they attributed negative characteristics to the Black dolls, saying they were ugly and nasty. Even though it was not a popular opinion in her time, today, psychologists and academics still agree with Cayton's assessment. In a recent interview with Maisonette's website, clinical psychologist Nanika Coor said, "When kids of color don't see themselves represented in media and toys, they don't feel valued, like something might be wrong with them." She emphasized that white children were also affected by the study. "White children are getting that same message—that kids of color don't belong in their worlds." However, many Black people felt there were more pressing issues in the Black community, such as discrimination and access to education. Perhaps they didn't understand that a child who feels valueless will have a difficult time navigating life.

Cayton's husband was a modern thinker for his time. He was very proud of his wife's writing career and her activism. He wrote in the *Seattle Republican* that Susie Cayton "was a woman who not only makes husbands men...but makes the men and women of tomorrow."

Revels Cayton was a talented author as well. Her short story "Sally the Egg-Woman" was published in the *Seattle P-I* on June 3, 1900. The characters she wrote about were richly developed. In 1902, her story "In the Land of Fire" was published. Its main character, Barkri, is a woman who grew up in a rural community in South America and discovers how cruel the community is. It was a place where the sick and old are sacrificed, old and useless women are handed over to cannibals and sick babies are thrown in fire pits. Cayton's story "The Part She Played" is the story of Mrs. Crosswaite, a woman grappling with life as a lonely wife suffering from anxiety and trying to hold an unhappy marriage together. Cayton's stories are rich in character development, and she used different races and cultures to enhance her characters.

Some people thought Cayton's stories were autobiographical because she had sustained several personal tragedies in a short time. In 1900, Cayton's sister Lillie died. Lillie had a daughter named Emma, who the Caytons decided to raise. Just six months later, Cayton's father died, and within weeks, her mother died. Her husband accompanied her to Mississippi and returned to Seattle after the deaths only to get into an altercation with the Seattle police chief. Cayton had printed a story criticizing the corruption of Mayor Thomas J. Humes's administration and his police chief, William Meredith. Meredith had Cayton tried for criminal libel. The family endured a lengthy trial, and Cayton was eventually acquitted of the charges.

Revels Cayton was also a busy clubwoman who was involved with many charities and cultural organizations. She was vice-president of the Negro Workers Club. She was one of the Dorcas Charity Club's founders. The club was formed to address what to do about a set of abandoned twins who were suffering from rickets. She was able to find a home for the twins. After that, the club tried to address the needs of Seattle's most impoverished Black residents. It raised money for widows and the sick and even gave toys to poor and orphaned children. When a young Black girl contracted tuberculosis, she received treatment at the children's hospital. The young girl needed ongoing treatment, and her stay at the hospital was longer than expected. Many hospitals practiced discrimination based on race and turned away patients who did not have money to pay. Susie Revels and the Dorcas Club worked with the founders of the Seattle Children's Hospital to treat all sick children regardless of their race or ability to pay. According to the Seattle Civil Rights and History Project's website, this is one of Revels Cayton's lasting legacies. Revels Cayton joined with other activists, such as Nettie Asberry, the founder of the Tacoma chapter of the NAAP, combining the

THE SEATTLE REPUBLICAN

This House for Rent 516 Fourteenth Ave. North Inquire at 307 Epler Block Main 305 or East 140

The Cayton House, circa 1909. In 2021, the Seattle Landmark Board approved the nomination of the house as a historic landmark. Photograph courtesy of the Seattle Republican/ Seattle Archives.

clubs to form the Washington State Association of Colored Women. The clubwomen became powerful voices for change.

The Caytons were an enigma to some in the Black community. During those early years in Seattle, most Black people lived in the Central District due to redlining. However, the Caytons lived on Capitol Hill, had servants and were surrounded by white neighbors, which didn't sit well with some Black residents in Seattle. Some even resented the Caytons, thinking they were trying to separate themselves from the average Black person. Some of their white neighbors were not thrilled with the living arrangement either. One white neighbor filed a lawsuit, arguing that his property value had decreased because a Black family had moved into the neighborhood. The Caytons won the case.

In 1909, the couple sold their Capital Hill house and purchased a home on East James Street. After their newspaper folded, the Caytons fell on hard times. Both had to take menial jobs. Revels worked as a domestic to make ends meet. Horace Cayton died in 1940. After his death, Susie Cayton moved to Chicago to live with one of her children. One of her sons had introduced her to the Communist Party; she joined and remained a member for the rest of her life.

Susie Revels Cayton died in 1943. She was a woman who defied her time's norms. She was a Black woman who had no history of enslavement. She was an educated woman, a working mother, a woman who worked in the newspaper industry and a lifelong activist who made life better and equitable for Black Americans during the early twentieth century.

In 1992, the Cayton Scholarship was created to benefit minority students. The Caytons taught their children to respect education and fight institutionalized racism. Horace Jr. was a prominent sociologist, newspaper columnist and author. Revels was a civil rights leader, and their daughter Madge was one of the first Black Americans to graduate from the University of Washington and became a social worker.

2

NETTIE CRAIG ASBERRY

Iconic Civil Rights Leader

Nettie Craig Asberry was a political activist, the founder of the Tacoma NAACP and the first Black woman to earn a doctorate. She was a civil rights activist who fought against racism and championed women's rights.

Nettie Craig Asberry was intelligent, caring and fearless—a true pioneer and trailblazer in an unkind and even cruel world to women of color. She was one of Tacoma's most respected and iconic citizens. Asberry is believed to be the first Black woman to earn a doctorate, was a founding member of the Tacoma chapter of the NAACP, a beloved music teacher and, later, a volunteer social worker.

Asberry was born in Leavenworth, Kansas, on July 15, 1865. Her mother, Violet Craig, was an enslaved woman who had six children. Her father, William Wallingford, was her mother's white slaveholder. Asberry was the youngest, and with the passage of the Emancipation Proclamation, Asberry was the first free person born in her family.

Asberry was an active member of the women's suffrage movement. Asberry's interest in women's rights began at an early age. At thirteen years old, she went to a rally and heard a speech by women's rights activist Susan B. Anthony. She was intrigued. She even became a secretary for one of the Susan B. Anthony clubs. She spent a great deal of her life fighting for women's (especially Black women's) rights. Asberry believed women had the right to an education and the right to work.

Eleanor Roosevelt once said, "The future belongs to those who believe in the vision of their dreams." Asberry embraced that philosophy. She always had great aspirations for herself. Bolstered by the idea of equality for women, Asberry enrolled in college and broke glass ceilings for Black women and, for that matter, all women. In 1883, she enrolled in college at the University of Kansas, something few Black Americans and even fewer Black women did in the 1880s. She always had a passion for music and began playing the piano at eight years old; she even composed her own music. So, it's no surprise that she earned her doctorate in music from the Kansas Conservatory of Music and Elocution in Leavenworth.

After graduation, she taught in the town of Nicodemus, Kansas. Black Americans founded Nicodemus in 1877 during the Reconstruction era after the Civil War. Many Black Americans wanted to escape from their memories of enslavement; one way was to migrate west. Many Black Americans took advantage of the Homestead Act of 1862. President Lincoln signed the Homestead Act into law on May 20, 1862, making it possible for free Black people to own their own land. The act allowed any American, including the formerly enslaved, to claim federal land (up to 160 acres).

Nettie Craig Asberry was a political activist and the founder of the Tacoma NAACP in 1913. Dr. Asberry is believed to be the first Black woman to earn a doctorate. She was a civil rights activist who fought against racism and championed women's rights. *Courtesy of UW Special Collections (ph coll. 663.1).*

Asberry's first husband was Albert Jones. They moved to Seattle in 1890. Unfortunately, Jones died shortly after in 1893, and Asberry returned to Kansas to be with her family. However, she soon returned to the Pacific Northwest and lived in Tacoma. It was in Tacoma where she met Henry Asberry. The two married on February 23, 1895. Henry Asberry was a successful barber at Gottleib Yaeger Barbershop at the Tacoma Hotel on 915 A Street. He was known as the barber to the stars, with such notable clients as Vice President Calvin Coolidge and Mark Twain, who stayed at the hotel while visiting Puget Sound for several weeks, and prominent local businesspeople.

A longtime civil rights activist, Nettie Asberry founded the Tacoma chapter of the National Association for the Advancement of Colored People (NAACP) in 1913, the oldest and largest civil rights organization in the United States. The Tacoma chapter was the first NAACP chapter west of the Mississippi. Asberry proved to be a mighty social justice warrior. The Washington State legislature had secretly rushed through a measure outlawing interracial marriage. Asberry got word of the secret meeting, and overnight, she organized a multiracial motorcade that crashed the legislature's session in protest. Their effort was successful, and the bill was easily defeated.

Asberry led a protest against racial segregation at Fort Lewis's military base. Segregation had actively been practiced in the military since the American Revolution. Black Americans and other minorities lived in separate quarters, often worked in support roles and ate in different dining facilities. Asberry reasoned that minority soldiers bravely served their country and put their lives on the line; therefore, all the soldiers should receive equal treatment. As a result, President Truman ended racial segregation in the military in 1948.

Asberry also opposed the practice of segregated seating in public places, such as movie theaters. Black people were relegated to sitting in the balcony in movie theaters, while white patrons occupied the floor seats. Asberry organized a letter-writing campaign for theater managers. Overwhelmed with letters, the managers dropped their segregation policy.

In 1915, famed movie director D.W. Griffith released his controversial movie titled *The Birth of a Nation*. Asberry described Griffith's screenplay as a three-hour propaganda crusade against the Reconstruction era and freed people after the Civil War. The movie depicted Black people as subhumans, buffoons, menacing and lustful, with the Ku Klux Klan finally coming to the rescue of white people.

Ellen Scott, the author of *Cinema Civil Rights*, wrote, "But for all its magnificence, what is inescapable in any assessment of *The Birth of a Nation* is the troubling racism that leaps off the screen. The film is one of the most racist films ever made, maybe the most racist film ever made." Asberry heard about the film and decided to see it while visiting Oakland, California. Predictably, she was disgusted by the portrayal; anger engulfed her body as she left the theater.

When Asberry learned that the film would be shown in Tacoma, she organized meetings with Black leaders, churches and civic groups to discuss their options. The movie, however, was a commercial success and was even shown at the White House for President Woodrow Wilson. But it had garnered protest across the country, and Tacoma was no exception. They organized protests, and Asberry was selected to write a protest letter to the *Tacoma Ledger*, published on August 13, 1916. A sentence from her letter read: "Protest meetings were held all over the city by whites and colored people." White ministers opened their churches to the public and preached powerful sermons against the immoral film. Theaters still showed the movie, but the protests might have scored a victory— the movie quickly disappeared from Tacoma theaters.

Asberry was known as a clubwoman. She organized many clubs aimed at Black women and designed to help them improve themselves. In 1908, she formed the Clover Leaf Art Club. The club brought in women from various clubs for "self-help activism." The club sponsored

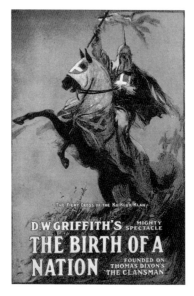

Dr. Asberry was appalled by *The Birth of a Nation* and organized protests to stop theaters from showing the film. *Photograph courtesy of the New York Public Library.*

such activities as conducting etiquette classes, providing scholarships to Black women and promoting arts and crafts competitions. These activities gave club members confidence and poise. Asberry started the club when she learned of the Alaska-Yukon Pacific Exposition, which was taking place in Seattle in 1909. She thought it was an excellent opportunity for Black women to display their talents and get recognition for their needlework and crafts. It was not an easy task to raise money for exhibit space. Members of the Clover Leaf Club sold crafts and Black dolls to raise money. They raised the money, and the women's displays were a great success, even winning a gold medal overall. "The women took on a new life and spirit," she said. The following year, Asberry's sister Martha Townsend won a silver medal for a lace opera coat that Asberry loved and wore often.

Clubs for Black women grew exponentially in the Puget Sound area and beyond. In 1917, the Washington State Federation of Colored Women was founded, primarily due to the Clover Leaf Art Club's success. In 1917, the Washington State Federation of Colored Women was formed. The club was associated with the National Association of Colored Women, founded in Washington, D.C., in 1896. The Washington State Federation

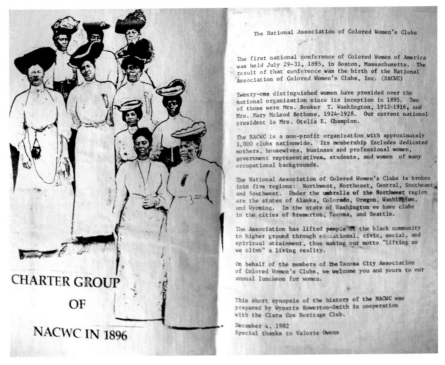

CHARTER GROUP

OF

NACWC IN 1896

The National Association of Colored Women's Clubs

The first national conference of Colored Women of America was held July 29–31, 1895, in Boston, Massachusetts. The result of that conference was the birth of the National Association of Colored Women's Clubs, Inc. (NACWC)

Twenty-one distinguished women have presided over the national organization since its inception in 1895. Two of those were Mrs. Booker T. Washington, 1912–1916, and Mrs. Mary McLeod Bethune, 1924–1928. Our current national president is Mrs. Otelia E. Champion.

The NACWC is a non-profit organization with approximately 1,000 clubs nationwide. Its membership includes dedicated mothers, housewives, business and professional women, government representatives, students, and women of many occupational backgrounds.

The National Association of Colored Women's Clubs is broken into five regions: Northwest, Northeast, Central, Southeast, and Southwest. Under the umbrella of the Northwest region are the states of Alaska, Colorado, Oregon, Washington, and Wyoming. In the state of Washington we have clubs in the cities of Bremerton, Tacoma, and Seattle.

The Association has lifted people of the black community to higher ground through educational, civic, social, and spiritual attainment, thus making our motto "Lifting as we climb" a living reality.

On behalf of the members of the Tacoma City Association of Colored Women's Clubs, we welcome you and yours to our annual luncheon for women.

This short synopsis of the history of the NACWC was prepared by Wynette Howerton-Smith in cooperation with the Clara Cox Heritage Club.

December 4, 1982
Special thanks to Valorie Owens

Asberry was a clubwoman and a prominent member of the Washington Association of Colored Women's Club. *Photograph courtesy of the Tacoma Association of Colored Women's Club.*

of Colored Women had more than 120 clubs with more than five hundred members. Some of the clubs included the Dorcas Charity Club, with fellow clubwoman Susie Revels Clayton. Black women did become powerful voices for change, and they gained a political voice because of the power of club participation. In an interview with the *Seattle P-I* Asberry said, "It would be uplifting to the colored children to know that their mothers and fathers helped make America what it is today." Asberry served as president of the Washington State Federation of Colored Women and was often requested to speak at events.

Asberry was committed to activism. In 1915, she was the founding member of the Tacoma chapter of the NAACP. She was also a member of the Tacoma Inter-Racial Council. Asberry said, "Courage is the saving grace in this tense world racial situation. The courage of the white people who dare to show their fairness by helping us achieve positions of human dignity; the courage of those of other races who risk insults by quietly asserting their rights as human beings."

Asberry became a symbol of justice and was a valued member of the community and a respected teacher. She gave private piano lessons to students and held more than forty-five music recitals a year. She taught hundreds of students of all races. Asberry also wanted her students to learn about Black history. She began teaching Black history to kids in her neighborhood and strongly suggested that schools devote some time in the school year to teach Black history. She was one of the best-known and most beloved teachers in Tacoma.

Asberry died in 1968 at 103 years old. She is remembered for her civil rights work and opening doors for women. Asberry is an icon in Tacoma. The city honored her with the Nettie Asberry Cultural Club Award as a way to preserve her memory. The Tacoma Association of Colored Women, which is still in existence, has four active clubrooms. One, the Asberry Cultural Club, is named in Nettie Craig Asberry's honor.

3

ALICE AUGUSTA BALL

Brilliant Unsung Chemist

Alice Ball discovered the first effective treatment for leprosy, which became known as the "Ball Method" and saved thousands of lives. Unfortunately, after her death, her work was stolen by a colleague, and it took decades before history was corrected.

Alice Augusta Ball was a brilliant chemist and medical researcher who, in 1916, discovered the first successful treatment for leprosy (Hansen's disease). Known as the the "Ball Method," her discovery was a major medical breakthrough, saved thousands of lives and released thousands more from leprosy colonies. However, because her work was stolen by a colleague, it was not known or credited to her for years.

Ball was also the first woman and the first Black American to receive her master's degree in chemistry from the University of Hawaii. She was also the first woman to teach chemistry at the university.

Alice Augusta Ball was born on July 24, 1982, in Seattle, Washington, to middle-class parents. Her mother, Laurie, was a photographer; her father, James P. Ball Jr., was a lawyer, photographer and editor of the *Colored Citizen*, a Black newspaper in Seattle. Ball was the third of four children, with two older brothers, Robert and William, and a younger sister, Addie. Her grandfather James Ball Sr. was an abolitionist and a well-known photographer. He was one of the first photographers to use the daguerreotype process of printing photographs. The method used various chemical solutions to print pictures on metal plates.

Left: Alice Ball discovered the first effective treatment for leprosy, which became known as the "Ball Method." *Photograph courtesy of the University of Hawaii.*

Right: Ball's grandfather James Ball was one of the first Black photographers to use daguerreotype photography. *Public domain.*

The family moved to Hawaii when Alice was a young child. James Ball Sr. had severe and painful arthritis; the family thought a warmer climate would help his condition. They only lived there for a year, because shortly after moving there, James Ball Sr. died. The family returned to Seattle.

While attending Seattle High School, Ball excelled in her studies, especially science and chemistry. She was a standout student. After graduating in 1910, there was no question that she would pursue a college education.

Ball was accepted to the University of Washington in 1910. Alice Ball obviously had confidence and support. In 1910, there were only 2,200 Black Americans attending the university. Black women were rarely educated, and it was even rarer that they would work in professional jobs. Although the white students avoided her, Ball was undaunted by the prejudices of the times. She continued to soar academically. Ball earned a bachelor's degree in pharmaceutical chemistry in 1912, and she returned to the university and received another degree in pharmacy science. She impressed her professors so much that one of her pharmacy professors asked her to coauthor a ten-page article titled "Benzoylations in Ether Solutions" in the *Journal of the American Chemical Society*, a prestigious scientific journal.

After graduation, Ball was flooded with scholarship offers to attend graduate school. She received offers from the University of California Berkeley and the University of Hawaii. She chose the University of Hawaii (then known as the College of Hawaii), perhaps remembering her time there as a child.

Ball received her master's degree. Her thesis was titled "The Chemical Constituents of Piper Methysticum; The Chemical Constituents of the Active Principle of the Kava Root." Her research involved isolating active ingredients in the kava root. This research drew Dr. Harry T. Hollmann's attention.

Dr. Hollmann worked with leprosy patients in the colonies in Hawaii. Leprosy is an infectious, debilitating and disfiguring disease that can damage the nerves, skin, eyes and respiratory system. One of the most recognizable symptoms are disfiguring skin sores. Those affected were stigmatized, isolated and sent to colonies, where they lived the rest of their lives. Leprosy had baffled doctors and scientists for hundreds of years. Hollmann researched an effective treatment using the chaulmoogra tree seed's properties, specifically the oil from the seed that could help treat the disease. The problem was finding a way to administer the medicine. Hollmann noticed that Ball's work with the kava root shared some of the same concepts. He reached out to her, and Ball was eager to take on the challenge. The problem with the treatment had been that when taken orally or injected, it had only exacerbated the condition. The medicinal taste made the patients throw up, and the injections were painful since the active ingredient was chaulmoogra acid.

Professor Ball worked tirelessly, and through a series of experiments, she isolated the essential oil needed and made a water-soluble solution that made the medication injectable. It resulted in the first successful treatment for leprosy. The treatment was later named after her and called the Ball Method. The treatment was used worldwide, relieving suffering and saving thousands of lives. Patients were able to leave hospitals and colonies and return home to their families. It was a triumph for the young professor, who was only twenty-three years old. Leprosy was treated with the Ball Method for more than thirty years until new treatments were developed in the 1940s.

Unfortunately, tragedy befell Professor Alice Ball before she could publish her lifesaving work. She became ill after accidentally inhaling chlorine gas during a lab demonstration. Ball returned home to Seattle for treatment. She returned to teaching before dying on December 31, 1916. A newspaper cited her cause of death as chlorine poisoning.

After Ball's death, Dr. Howard Dean, the president of the University of Hawaii, found her research and took credit for her work. He mass-produced Ball's discovery and shipped it around the world.

It was not until 1922, when Ball's former collegue Dr. Hollmann wrote a paper detailing Ball's discovery and work in developing a treatment for leprosy and other diseases that the treatment was attributed to her. He called her discovery the Ball Method. The article did little to give Ball her proper recognition. Dean was still heralded as a medical hero for curing a disease that had affected and baffled so many for hundreds of years. He became the rock star of medicine in newspapers, magazines and medical journals.

However, in the 1970s, Dr. Kathryn Takara, a writer at the University of Hawaii, discovered Ball's name, started investigating her contribution and brought her work to light again. Finally, Alice Ball was given credit for her brilliant work.

In 2000, the University of Hawaii dedicated a plaque in Ball's name and placed it under the only chaulmoogra tree on campus to the right some of the wrongs. Also in 2000, the lieutenant governor of Hawaii Mazie Hirono declared February 29 Alice Ball Day, and it is now celebrated every four years. In 2007, Ball was granted the Medal of Distinction.

In 2017, Paul Wermager, a scholar who lectures and publishes pieces about Ball, created a scholarship in her name. The Alice Augusta Ball Scholarship was established for students pursuing studies in chemistry, biology or microbiology.

In 2000, the World Health Organization declared that leprosy was no longer a global health problem.

Alice Augusta Ball defied the limitations of racism and sexism in the Jim Crow era to become a brilliant scientist and chemist. Her discovery relieved the pain, suffering, isolation and stigmatization of thousands of leprosy patients. She accomplished so much in her twenty-four years of life.

4

WASHINGTON STATE FEDERATION OF COLORED WOMEN'S CLUBS

The Washington State Federation of Colored Women's Club was founded by Black women in 1917. The club's purpose was to better Black Americans' social, economic and political conditions.

On June 25, 1924, Jennie Samuels, the Washington State Federation of Colored Women's Clubs president, welcomed more than two thousand club members to the club's state convention. Samuels, the second president of the club, had an ambitious agenda for the three-day event. Scheduled were arts-and-crafts exhibits and seminars on how the club could improve the lives of the Black community, temperance and even interracial relations. "It is our duty, as representatives of colored people of the state, to do all in our power to assume our true position in the life of the nation," said Samuels in her opening remarks.

Clubwomen became a force to be reckoned with during the late 1800s and early 1900s. Aside from their social activism to improve the plight of Black people, especially women and children, the clubwomen were often powerful forces in politics. As evidence of that, Everett's mayor John Henry Smith and former mayor and future Washington governor Roland H. Hartley were keynote speakers at the convention, according to the *Everett Herald*, which covered the event.

The Washington State Federation of Colored Women's Clubs was formed on August 9, 1917. Women from more than 120 clubs across the state met at the home of Mrs. George Clay in Spokane, Washington. Another purpose

Early presidents of the Washington State Federation of Colored Women's Clubs. *Photograph courtesy of the Tacoma Association of Colored Women's Clubs.*

of the gathering was to seek affiliation with the National Association of Colored Women's Clubs. The national organization was known for its high standards for membership, and the Washington State club was confident that its goals aligned. Both clubs' main goal was the economic and social betterment of Black women and children.

The Black women's clubs of the 1890s focused on social and political concerns. Local chapters, like those in Washington, launched civil rights campaigns strongly opposing segregation and supporting antilynching legislations. Women like Ida B. Wells and Mary McLeod Bethune advocated for the right to an education for Black children, the right to vote and antilynching campaigns.

The National Association of Colored Women's Clubs was founded in July 1896. Its motto was: "Lifting As We Climb." The club was founded in response to a vile, racist letter written by a southern journalist, James Jacks. He claimed that Black women were thieves, prostitutes and liars, among other disrespectful descriptions. Mary Church Terrell and Josephine St. Pierre Ruffin, two formally educated Black women, were incensed at

The clubwomen focused on "racial uplift." The club's motto is: "Today is ours for united service." Photograph circa 1924. *Photograph courtesy of the Tacoma Association of Colored Women's Clubs.*

the attack on the morals and respectability of Black women and decided to organize. Mary Terrell said, "Too long have we been silent under unjust and unholy charges. We cannot expect to have them removed until we disprove them through ourselves." They sent out requests to a virtual who's who of some of the most prominent Black women in the country. In addition to Terrell and St. Pierre Ruffin, the founders included Harriet Tubman, the well-known abolitionist; Ida B. Wells, noted publisher, journalist and a leader of the antilynching movement; Mary McLeod Bethune, educator, civil rights activist and advisor to four United States presidents; Frances E.W. Harper, poet, suffragist, writer and teacher; and Margaret Murray Washington, principal of the Tuskegee Normal and Industrial Institute (later Tuskegee University) and the third wife of Booker T. Washington, the famous educator, author and orator.

Black women have always come together to establish clubs, usually centered on improving the living conditions of Black women and children. The clubs traditionally partnered with Black churches to get resources to lift Black Americans out of poverty.

The two main organizers, Mary Church Terrell and Josephine St. Pierre Ruffin, were well-established women. Terrell was one of the first Black women to earn a college degree (at Oberlin College) and was a national civil rights activist. In an inspirational speech about Black women, she said, "Colored women have always had high aspirations for themselves and their race from the day when shackles fell from their fettered limbs till today. As

The Spokane chapter of the Washington State Federation of Colored Women's Club, 1917. *Photograph courtesy of the Tacoma Association of Colored Women's Club.*

individuals, they have often struggled single-handed and alone against the most desperate and discouraging odds."

Josephine St. Pierre Ruffin was a publisher, journalist and civil rights leader. She published a national newspaper, the *Women's Era*, geared toward Black women.

The Washington Federation of Colored Women's Clubs' motto was: "Today is Ours for United Service." The club was known for education and training programs for low-income Black women.

Cynthia Tucker, the current president of the Tacoma chapter, said, "We're almost as old as the national branch, and that's because women like Nettie Asberry believed in unity. They addressed the needs of the Black family, and our present-day club carries on that legacy." Tucker said the women before were concerned with lynching, voting rights, educating Black children and living wherever they wanted. Tucker said some of those issues are still very present today. "We are still fighting discrimination," said Tucker.

Today, the Washington Association of Colored Women's Club (WACWC) continues the work of those who came before, especially with children. "We try to educate children about our history," explained Tucker. "For example, we do a Kwanza program. We have a luncheon, and a speaker comes in to explain the meaning of Kwanza," said Tucker. "In January, the club puts on a Martin Luther King Jr. program. February is our Black History Month program. We pick specific topics to discuss, such as the Tulsa Massacre. We try to educate the public as well as children about Black history."

Tucker explained what drew her to the club and why she became a member. "I'm originally from Pennsylvania. I was a military wife, and we traveled a lot," she explained. When she moved to Washington State, she heard of the WACWC. "I felt the need to be in the company of other Black women. There are so many things we can learn from other Black women—from raising children to education to life's lessons," she said. "I think Black women's experiences are unique. Wherever I have been, I am a Black woman. That's why it is important for me to keep the club going."

Tucker organized and hosted the 2019 convention. It included clubs from three states, Washington, Alaska and Oregon (the Northwest Region), and lasted five days. "It was a fantastic event, and it went off perfectly," she said. Tucker said they had arts-and-crafts exhibits, as they did at very early conventions.

Cynthia Tucker is the current president and historian of the Tacoma Association of Colored Women's Club. *Photograph courtesy of Cynthia Tucker.*

Tucker said the club's membership has waned over the years. "Women have a lot going on in their lives today," she said. But Tucker is convinced that the WACWC will continue to exist because women will always need other women.

Tucker is proud that the Tacoma chapter is still active and adheres to the mission to promote education, health and cultural awareness.

The club's current works include:

1. Bringing people together to deliberate and celebrate.
2. Providing a hub for civic service groups, such as the Black Collective, Tees and Turf Golf Club and the Black Women's Political Caucus.
3. Increasing awareness and appreciation of Black history and culture.
4. Providing a "central gathering place" for the community.

Tucker said the Tacoma chapter had attained several accomplishments. Former club president Bertie Edwards started a senior citizen awareness day that became a Tacoma Senior Services division model. The club owned and operated a seniors crafts store.

Before she passed away, Washington State club president and historian Freddie May Barnett shared her memories of past club presidents (she didn't know the first four presidents) with current Tacoma president and historian Cynthia Tucker. Barnett joined the club in 1959. "I joined the Washington Association of Colored Women's Clubs because I wanted to be as active in

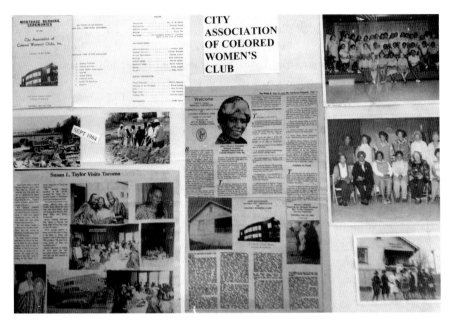

The Washington State Federation of Colored Women's Club encouraged women to develop skills to improve their life. *Photograph courtesy of the Tacoma Association of Colored Women's Club.*

this community as I was in the military community [her husband was in the military]," said Barnett.

Barnett remembers Dr. Nettie Asberry as a great activist. "I learned so much from her. She fought so hard for the community on racial issues. She stood up for the rights of African Americans in the state," she told Tucker. "She taught piano to all races because she wanted to ensure that all people of all races had the opportunity to learn music and be treated equally. That was her passion," she said.

Barnett described Mrs. Eliza Champ-McCabe as a passionate teacher. McCabe graduated from a college in Texas with a teaching degree before moving to Tacoma. "After moving to Tacoma from Texas, she could not get a job as a teacher in Washington, even though she had her degree and experience in teaching. It was because she was Black," said Barnett. "Like Dr. Asberry, she taught music by giving private lessons in her home. She wanted everyone to speak correctly at all times." Barnett described McCabe as meticulous and said she ensured the club's meetings were "carried out properly and in order." McCabe was a clubwoman through and through, according to Barnett. She organized many clubs in Tacoma, including the Bethune Woman's Christian Temperance Union and McCabe Twenty. "She also helped Bremerton establish their club," she said. Mrs. McCabe also wrote the club's prayer. "The prayer continues to be the opening prayer of every Washington Sister Club meeting," said Barnett. According to the *Washington State Association of Colored Women's Clubs' News* (April 1979), McCabe was given the key to the city of Tacoma by Mayor Mike Parker. She also received birthday greetings from the President Jimmy Carter and Rosalynn Carter.

Helen Stafford was the first Black social worker for the state. She was also the first Black supervisor for the Washington Department of Social Services. Stafford was a teacher before moving to Tacoma. "Her race blocked her from being a teacher, so she became a social worker. She was an advocate for change and fought for civil rights and women's rights," said Barnett. Barnett said Stafford had many firsts in Tacoma as a Black woman. "She was also the first Black member of Tacoma's League of Women Voters. Although she wasn't allowed to teach, she eventually received an honorary 'doctrine of humanitarian service degree' from the University of Puget Sound. It was well deserved," said Barnett.

Barnett said Dr. Asberry, Mrs. McCabe and Mrs. Stafford were instrumental in organizing peaceful protests and attending legislative meetings in Olympia, voicing their opinions about discrimination in Tacoma.

In 2005, Tacoma named an elementary school after Mrs. Stafford, Helen B. Stafford Elementary School.

Barnett also remembered Mrs. Arline Yarbrough, a former president and historian. "She loved our Black club history. Mrs. Yarbrough had all the members write their biographies," she said.

Barnett said during the 1970s, Mrs. Elizabeth Westley focused on hunger and feeding the community. "Food banks were not readily available at that time. Mrs. Westley worked with her church; Shiloh Baptist Church fed anyone hungry—no one was turned away."

"Mrs. Bertie Edwards, with the help of her husband and the community, raised enough funds to build a new clubhouse," said Barnett. "Mrs. Edwards also organized the city's first senior citizens center."

Mrs. Clare Cox-Sharon was instrumental in constructing the parking lot. "Her idea was to sell pavement bricks with the buyers' names engraved on as many bricks as they wanted; it was a success," said Barnett. Tucker said some of the bricks remain today.

Barnett herself wanted to preserve the past and organized a yearly fundraiser for the Asberry Scholarship Award, which was started under Dr. Asberry.

Addie Rose Dunlap was one of Seattle's most dedicated club members, according to Barnett. "She was the club's photographer and journalist," said Barnett. "She does not miss any conventions in the state or out of state. Her passion and dedication ensure that the history of the club is passed on to new members through her photography and newsletters. She also preserved anything historical about the club."

Barnett said Theda Morris and Matres Johnson were passionate about arts and crafts. "Arts and crafts were the staples of the original clubs," she said. "Mrs. Johnson made sure at every Colored Women's Clubs convention that craft items were present for display."

Barnett explained that many great women had been a part of the Washington Association of Colored Women's Clubs all over the state. "There are so many of them—in Seattle, there was Zelda Brown, Mildred Germon, Annette Shumate, Mrs. Ponder, Mrs. Kirk and Mrs. Purnell. In Yakima, there was Mrs. Bryant, and in Longview, there was Mrs. Victoria Freeman. In Bremerton, there was Mrs. Lillian Walker and Mrs. Grier. The passion of these women was phenomenal," said Barnett.

Cynthia Tucker said the Tacoma City Association of Colored Women's Clubs played a significant role in the election of the first-ever Black man running for president of the United States. "There was a rally held at the clubhouse, and John Kerry came to campaign for President Obama. There were many campaign rallies in Washington and inauguration parties all over the state. A big day in Black history was celebrated on November 6, 2008, as club members prepared for the first-ever Black president," said Tucker.

Washington's state club president Carol Mitchell said, "Today we dream anew.…We seek to maximize our contribution to community betterment by converting our clubhouse into a multicultural civic center that serves the entire South Puget Sound."

5

BERTHA PITTS CAMPBELL

Pioneering Activist and Trailblazer

Bertha Pitts Campbell was an iconic civil rights activist. She was one of the founders of the Delta Sigma Theta sorority while attending Howard University. Campbell was the first Black person to become a board member of the YWCA, making Seattle the first city to integrate the YWCA Board.

According to newspaper reports, it was a beautiful, crisp day on March 3, 1913, in Washington, D.C. Excitement filled the air. The day was particularly exhilarating for the Howard University senior Bertha Pitts. She and her fellow newly formed Delta Sigma Theta sorority members were there for the massive suffrage rally to fight for the right of women to vote.

In 1913, Pitts was one of twenty-two young women who had formed the Delta Sigma Theta sorority. The event was the first time the sorority made its political debut, and it was ready to fight for a just cause—the right for women to vote.

Bertha Pitts was born on June 30, 1889, in Winfield, Kansas. When she was a young girl, her family moved to Colorado. Pitts was the only Black student in her high school class in Montrose, Colorado. It was an unusual circumstance for the granddaughter of a former enslaved person. She was a brilliant student who was vivacious and loved to dance. She delivered the valedictorian address for her graduating class. Pitts was offered a full scholarship to Colorado College, but she turned it down for another option.

In 1908, she was accepted to Howard University, one of the nation's premier historical Black colleges and universities (HBCUs). It was an

Bertha Pitts Campbell was one of the founding members of the Delta Sigma Theta Sorority. *Photograph courtesy of the Delta Sigma Theta Sorority Incorporated®*.

exciting time for Pitts. She was meeting young Black women with whom she had so much in common.

Pitts and twenty-one of her fellow sisters from the Delta Theta Sigma sorority wanted more than a social organization; they wanted their sorority to pursue "the betterment of their race," according to the *Washington Post* article "Democracy Dies in Darkness" by Syndey Trent. The March 3 parade was an essential step in creating equality for Black women. Unfortunately, the Deltas were not listed in the program, which was a big disappointment. Ironically, in a march for women's equality, the Deltas, like other Black women, were relegated to the back of the parade by white organizers from the South. But the organizers were unaware of the grit of the Black women in attendance. On that historic day in 1913, the Deltas and other formidable women, like Ida B. Wells, ignored their designated segregated areas and blended in with other marchers.

Pitts graduated from Howard University in 1913 with a bachelor's degree in education and taught for two years in Topeka, Kansas. Her family, along with Pitts, returned to Colorado, where she met and married her husband, a railroad man named Earl Allen Campbell.

The couple moved to Seattle, Washington, in 1923. "We left Colorado because the war was over," said Pitts Campbell in her oral history interview with writer Esther Munford in 1975. "We thought the conditions would be better out here for work. My husband was a railroad man, and he decided that he'd like to change to something else. So, we came to Seattle looking for work."

The couple made their life in Seattle, living south of Jackson Street. Her husband got a job working in government service at the immigration station. He worked there until 1954, when he died of a heart attack. The Campbells had one son.

Pitts Campbell was an early civil rights worker in Seattle. She dedicated her life to many causes. Pitts Campbell said when she moved to Seattle, there were very few Black residents in town. "There were only about 2,500 to 3,000 negroes who lived here. When I first came here, there was no Urban

League. There were no organizations like that…all those things came later." The only organized institution for Black residents, according to Pitts Campbell, was the YWCA. She harkened back to her Howard University days and joined the Phyllis Wheatley branch of the YWCA and was an active member for fifty-three years. The Phyllis Wheatley branch was named after Phyllis Wheatley, the first Black woman and only the second woman to be a published author. Wheatley's work was a book of poetry titled *Poems on Various Subjects, Religious and Moral*. Wheatley was sold into slavery around eight years old and was taught to read and write by her slaveholder's daughter and son.

Pitts Campbell was the chair of the branch from 1932 to 1936. During her tenure, she was a formidable advocate for Black women and children in the Central District, providing critical services. The board of the YWCA often asked Pitts Campbell to speak or do presentations for the branch at board meetings. However, she wasn't allowed a vote because she was Black. Pitts Campbell, a longtime proponent of equality, insisted that depriving her of voting rights was unacceptable. Since she did the work of other board members, she insisted on having a say. Finally, the board relented, and in 1936, the Seattle YWCAs were the first in the nation to have an integrated board of directors.

In her oral history story, Pitts Campbell reflected on life in Seattle in the late 1920s: "We didn't have outright discrimination but several suggestions of it. Like for instance, offering to give the negroes a beach of their own. But we said, no, we don't need a beach with all the beaches that are around and in our neighborhood. We don't need a special beach.…So that died out, and we didn't have one." She saw many changes in her years living in Seattle. When she was a young woman, Black women could not eat in Frederick & Nelson's (Seattle's premier department store at that time) Tea Room, nor could they try personal items, such as gloves. But there were great places that welcomed everyone, she said. The Seattle Opera House, for example, was open to Black people, and there were no restrictions on where Black patrons could sit.

Pitts Campbell was the first Black woman to become a board member of the Seattle YWCA. *Photograph courtesy of the Black Heritage Society.*

During World War II, the city's landscape began to change. To help the war effort, Boeing and other companies had jobs available and needed people to fill them. So, people from all over the country came to Seattle to live and work. Many Black Americans moved from southern states to make a better life, and many of them were women. Boeing had hired many women, but they didn't have anywhere to stay. "We converted our recreation room in our building [at the YWCA] into a dormitory…and we kept them there until the end of the war," said Campbell.

Pitts Campbell was a devoted member of the First African Methodist Episcopal Church in Seattle. As a woman of deep faith, she thought working with other Christians of all races could help close the racial divide in the city. In 1942, Campbell joined with other Christian women and formed the Christian Friends for Racial Equality. The organization was an interracial group of Christians whose goal was to erase racial discrimination by applying the "golden rule" (do unto others as you would have done unto you) in tackling racial equality. One of the tenets stated: "We stand for equality and opportunity for all men of all races, the rights and privileges guaranteed by the Constitution and the Bill of Rights." It was a unique approach to activism. The organization sought to strengthen the bonds that unite people as one. In her oral history, Pitts Campbell said, "This was an interracial group, and you know, for a long time, we tried our best to find a place for an office.…We couldn't get a place rented to us for an office because it was an interracial group." However, with perseverance, the council found an office to rent and set out to eliminate segregation and discrimination in housing, restaurants, movie theaters and hotels, among other industries. Pitts Campbell said the organization achieved amazing results. For example, the Red Cross started training people of color. "The Red Cross trained three Negroes and one Chinese person as nurses' aides," she said. Before that, the Red Cross had refused to have Black people work in their organization as nurses' aides or to have them visit the troops as Gray Ladies. Campbell said the Christian Friends of Racial Equality kept pushing, and since the war was in full effect, the Red Cross finally relented. "Of course, I don't know why you'd have to be trained to go up and visit a boy and write a letter for him," said Pitts Campbell.

The Christian Friends of Racial Equality had many victories in its discrimination fights, especially in the area of housing. For example, there was a covenant in many real estate contracts that homeowners would agree not to sell to Black people. The Christian Friends of Racial Equality fought hard, and eventually, the covenant was declared illegal.

The Bertha Pitts Campbell Equity Awards honors the life of the trailblazer and those who work for equality. *Photograph courtesy of the YWCA/Seattle/King/Snohomish.*

The organization also fought for quality healthcare for Black people by working with hospitals to ensure physicians and hospitals were restricted from refusing services. When she was ninety-two, Pitts Campbell's activism came full circle. She led ten thousand Delta Sigma Theta sorority members along the same route of Pennsylvania Avenue in Washington, D.C.—the same route taken during the 1913 suffrage march.

Bertha Pitts Campbell died on April 2, 1990, at 101 years old. Her life was well lived and was service-oriented. On May 11, 1987, the Washington State House of Representatives honored Pitts Campbell for her work and life, and the City of Seattle proclaimed June 13, 1987, Bertha Pitts Campbell Day.

6

LILLIAN WALKER

Bremerton's Civil Rights Vanguard

Lillian Walker was one of the founders of the Bremerton NAACP
and worked to desegregate local businesses.

When Lillian Walker was in the third grade, one of her white classmates called her the N-word. According to her oral history story for the Legacy Washington Project, written by John Hughes, she recounted that she calmly handed her books to another classmate and proceeded to punch the girl in the nose. She and her siblings were the only Black students at the school. The girl, named Helen, never called her that word again, and the two became best friends. Even as a child, Lillian Walker had no qualms about standing up for human dignity and racial equality. It was a starting point for the woman who would become an iconic civil rights fighter in the city of Bremerton, Washington. Walker was one of the founders of the first NAACP branch in Bremerton. She and her husband, James Walker, worked diligently to desegregate local establishments in Kitsap County. She was also a founding board member of the YWCA in Bremerton.

She was born Lillian Allen on October 2, 1913, in Carrier Mills, Illinois, in a dilapidated shack with no electricity or running water. Lillian was one of eleven children born to mixed-race parents, Moses and Hazel Allen. Her grandmother Elvira Allen was reportedly the granddaughter of a Tennessee slave owner. Elvira apparently ran away and married a man of Portuguese descent, although the details of his background are vague. Elvira's second husband was Willis Allen, the son of a Black father and white mother. Lillian Walker's father was a farmer on a twenty-acre farm. The children were

Lillian married her husband, James, on June 20, 1941. The couple were civil rights activists. *Photograph courtesy of the Legacy Project, Washington Secretary of State.*

responsible for backbreaking chores on the farm, including hoeing, plowing, taking care of the animals and working the fields. Walker's family was dirt poor. She told Hughes in her oral history interview that when the Depression engulfed the country, they didn't even notice because nothing about their life was different.

Despite their circumstances, Lillian Walker's parents wanted more for their children. Education was important to the Allen family, as was religion. They insisted, in addition to their farm work, that their children attended school every day. Like most students in a rural area, the school was small, a two-room building. Lillian was a tenacious student. Teachers raved about her work; she excelled in every subject. Without electricity, she and her siblings were forced to read by a kerosene lamp at night. Their mother, Hazel, was an inspiration to Lillian. Hazel Allen had suffered a head injury at the hands of her stepfather that left her unable to read. Walker often read to her, and her mother enjoyed it. Walker said in her oral history that despite their hardships, her parents were never negative and always encouraged them to strive to be their best. "Dad always said you can do anything anybody else can do."

Lillian Walker grew up committed to her religious faith. Her parents insisted that their children attend church and live a Christian life. Walker recalled in her oral history that the entire family dressed in "their Sunday best" as they prepared for church. They didn't have much, but their clothes were clean and pressed. Her strong religious beliefs played a significant role in her fight for equal rights for all.

After graduating from high school, Walker wanted to become a doctor, but her family didn't have money, and her race and gender played a significant role in keeping her from that profession.

Walker still wanted a medical career and set her sights on nursing. She got a job at the Home Sanitorium in Harrisburg while taking nursing courses. She worked there for little more than two years before moving to Chicago in 1937 to live with her aunt.

In Chicago, Lillian Allen met her future husband, James T. Walker, a working musician who played the saxophone. According to her oral history

story, Walker was not interested in being the wife of a musician. She told her future husband, "I'm not going to marry a musician. I'll starve to death." James Walker assured his future wife that he wanted something more stable as well. The couple was married on June 20, 1941. They were married for fifty-nine years until James's death of natural courses at the age of eighty-nine. The two stood together and fought for racial equality.

James's mother lived in Seattle, Washington, home to the Boeing Company. They moved to Bremerton, where James got a job at the naval shipyard. The number of jobs in Washington State grew exponentially during Word War II, as did the need for people to work in them. During the war years (mainly 1940 to 1944), the population jumped from 15,000 to 75,000. Black people from all over the country, especially from the South, moved to Puget Sound to get good-paying jobs and seek a better life. In Bremerton, the racial demographics changed exponentially as well. Black Americans moved to the city to work at the naval shipyard. Before the war, approximately 100 Black people lived in Bremerton, and by 1944, that number had exploded to 4,600.

When the Walkers moved to Bremerton, it was a culture shock in a sense. Coming from Illinois, where they hadn't experienced such outright racism, it was disconcerting. Black people were greeted by "whites only" signs at several businesses, including taverns, cafés, barbershops, et cetera. In her oral history interview, Walker described Bremerton as a "white supremacist town." The Walkers and other Black people were subjected to blatant racism, something Lillian Walker was bound and determined to end. Black people were often assaulted or arrested for just standing around. The Walkers were outraged and decided something needed to be done.

Lillian Walker joined the Puget Sound Civil Society, a civil rights organization, and became its recording secretary. However, the racism was so pervasive that the Walkers decided a more robust response was needed. They had their own experience with racism at a barbershop where James went to get a haircut. Walker explained that the barber told them to come back after 5:00 p.m., and he would close the shades and cut his hair. In her oral history story, Lillian said, "If he couldn't cut a Black man's hair in broad daylight, there was no way we were going to go back there." Lillian told her husband that she would be cutting his hair from then on, as well as their son's and her brother's, who had come to live in Bremerton to work at the shipyards. The Walkers had two children: Jimmy was born in 1945, and June was born in 1950.

The city of Bremerton and Kitsap County at that time were steeped in Jim Crow–like laws. With discriminatory hiring practices, housing restrictions and redlining and segregation, the Walkers and other prominent community members, such as Reverend Chester Cooper, who was pastor of Ebenezer AME Church, founded the first branch of the NAACP in Bremerton. In a Historylink.org article, Walker said, "I knew that you would have all races fighting for civil rights with the NAACP." So, she contacted the Seattle branch of the NAACP, and she was right. They had access to resources and more people willing to fight the good fight.

Lillian Walker later became the state secretary of the NAACP. Meanwhile, the Bremerton branch started the arduous task of dismantling segregation one step at a time. First, Walker was right about many other races joining in and supporting the desegregation cause in Bremerton. Then, in her oral history interview, she recalled two personal incidences. First, she cited her neighbor Ron Johnson, who offered his protection and said he was standing by the Walkers if anyone tried to attack them. Then, Peggy Gustafson backed Walker when a waitress at a café took Gustafson's order and ignored Mrs. Walker. The waitress called the police, who determined that Walker had done nothing wrong by wanting to be served at the café.

The NAACP mobilized to eliminate the "white only" signs in businesses throughout Bremerton and Kitsap County. In addition, the Walkers organized sit-ins at cafés, taverns and other institutions that practiced segregation. Walker also organized protest marches, which Martin Luther King Jr. and civil rights protestors used effectively during the 1960s. Little by little, the relics of racial segregation began disappearing. Finally, a critical victory was won when, in 1949, the Fair Employment Practices Act was passed. Fair employment and fair housing were two primary components of the Walkers' equal rights campaign.

You would think that the end of the war would bring about new beginnings, but there were still fights to be won. One fight involved James Walker personally. In 1954, he tried to buy a cup of coffee at a drugstore in Bremerton, and the owner refused and called him a racial epithet. The owner obviously didn't realize that Walker was a longtime fighter for equality. So, Walker contacted a civil rights attorney. Walker and a friend returned to the drugstore, the owner again refused them service and Walker promptly filed a civil rights complaint. It was a tough battle, but the owner finally settled by taking down his "whites only" sign and agreeing to serve everyone.

The Walkers were committed parents who were very involved in the PTA and, of course—one of the cornerstones of their upbringing—the church. They were active members of Ebenezer AME Church. The church often joined the NAACP in organizing protests and sit-ins.

Lillian Walker intended to make Bremerton a better place to live for its residents throughout her life. So in 1947, she and a group of other women founded the YWCA of Kitsap County. In her oral history interview, Walker described the development of the YWCA as a labor of love. She said that the YWCA became an essential part of "the social fabric" of the community. The younger and older women could take classes on everything "from exercise, to etiquette, to self-defense." She was also instrumental in the development of a regional library system. As a strong proponent of education, Lillian Walker became chairperson of the regional library board.

Lillian's husband, James Walker, died at the age of eighty-nine in 2000. The couple had been married for fifty-nine years. In her oral history interview, she said of James, "If I had searched the world over, I couldn't have found a better mate." Lillian Walker continued her community work until her death on January 4, 2012. She was ninety-eight years old. In her obituary, which was printed in the *Kitsap Sun* newspaper, Linda Joyce, who was executive director at the Kitsap YWCA, said, "There are some people who are born to make a difference in this world. Some are born with that degree of tenacity." Lillian made many friends during her life, and one was appeals court judge Robin Hunt, who shared in the obituary, "She was tenacious as a bulldog disguised in velvet. She was feisty but never mean." Judge Hunt continued, "She had a wonderful, remarkable life and was quite an example to so many people."

It's incalculable the amount of influence Walker had on others in her life. "We have turned to her throughout the past sixty years. She is the soul of this community."

Lillian Walker was one of those "hidden figures" in our history who laid her life on the line in many instances, all intending to make life better for others. She had a full and long life.

Walker was honored with many awards during her life, among them is the Golden Acorn Award from the PTA. The YWCA presented her with the Founder's Award. The Democrats presented her with the Lifetime Achievement Award, and the National Association of Colored Women's Club gave her the Mary Terrell Lifetime Achievement Award. She was honored to receive the Liberty Bell Award from the Kitsap County Bar Association.

Lillian Walker was survived by her children, grandchildren, great-grandchildren and extended family. Her friends and family said that her accolades humbled her, but she was a force that initiated change for the better. Her friend Judge Hunt described her as "the living embodiment of Lincoln's Emancipation Proclamation and Martin Luther King's dream. She accomplished this without rancor, but rather, with an attitude that others needed to be educated."

7

THELMA DEWITTY

Seattle's First Black Teacher

Thelma Dewitty broke two barriers when she was hired as a teacher in 1947. She was the first Black woman to be a teacher in Seattle and the first married woman to become a teacher for the school board.

In 1947, Thelma Fisher Dewitty walked into Frank B. Cooper Elementary School as the Seattle School Board's first Black teacher. She wasn't sure what the reception would be. In her oral history story for the Legacy History Project with writer Esther Mumford, she described it as very cordial. "It was later told to me that the principal had told the other teachers when I would arrive, and if any of them objected to working with a Black person, they could leave," she said.

Thelma Fisher Dewitty was born in Beaumont, Texas, in 1912. She had been an excellent student and graduated from Wiley College in Marshall, Texas, in 1941. Dewitty was the perfect candidate to break the color barrier; she had all the qualifications to teach in the Seattle school system. She had her bachelor's degree from an accredited college, she had passed the state's approved program and she had considerable teaching experience.

Wanting to join her husband on August 11, she called the school board and asked about a teaching position. "I was just thinking about getting an appointment for the next year," she said in an article for the *Seattle P-I* in 1947. Instead, the board gave her an application, and on August 30, she was notified that she was hired.

She was an accomplished teacher with fourteen years of teaching experience under her belt. Dewitty first taught in Corpus Christi, Texas, for nine years and in Beaumont, Texas, for five years.

Top: Dewitty's original application to the Seattle Public Schools. *Courtesy of Seattle Public Schools' archives.*

Bottom: Article from the *Seattle P-I* announcing the hiring of Dewitty. *Courtesy of Seattle Public Schools' archives.*

During the summer of 1947, Dewitty attended the University of Washington, studying for her master's degree. She had visited her husband in Seattle for the last few summers because the retired army veteran worked at Seattle's Port of Embarkation. Dewitty wanted to move to Seattle and work as a teacher full time to be with her husband, but Seattle had never hired a Black teacher. Many Black people who had graduated with teaching degrees had to leave the state if they wanted to work as teachers, so her prospects seemed bleak.

After the war, the racial demographics for Seattle and other parts of Washington State had evolved. There were more minorities and more civil rights organizations fighting for equal access to jobs. Many civil rights organizations, such as the NAACP and the Christian Friends for Racial Equality, urged the school board to hire someone who was Black.

Dewitty's first assignment was teaching at Frank B. Cooper Elementary School for six years. "I was told when I came that they wanted me to

Dewitty's first teaching assignment was with Cooper Elementary School. *Photograph courtesy of Seattle Public Schools' archives.*

move around," she explained in her oral history story. She also taught at Laurelhurst, Sandpoint, John Bay and Meany Junior High. "I think I had more visits from parents than any other teacher in the school," she said in her oral history story. Her students loved her and often brought her flowers.

Most of the parents were happy with the way Dewitty taught their children. But there was one incident that Dewitty recounted in her oral history. One mother was from the South, and when she visited the school and met Dewitty, she immediately went to the principal and said she didn't know the teacher was Black and demanded that her child be moved to another room. The principal was adamant and told the mother that her daughter would not be moved and that she was no longer in the South. Dewitty had the principal's full support, and he recounted that he told the mother the only way her daughter would be moved out of Dewitty's classroom was if she moved out of the neighborhood. Dewitty said the story had a happy ending; at the end of the school year, the mother told Dewitty how glad she was that her daughter had learned so much in her class.

After that, Dewitty said there weren't any complaints from parents about her teaching. Dewitty noted in her oral history story that parents of students frequently invited her to their homes. As for her fellow teachers, she said she had primarily professional and cordial relationships. "I came in and said good morning. If they asked me a question, I answered, and I was friendly.... Those who wanted to invite me over, I accepted and then had them over."

Although her work life was free of racial strife, the same cannot be said of her personal life. She said in her oral history that when she and her husband bought their first house in a white neighborhood, they were constantly harassed. "I hate to think about it. They would park their cars in my driveway. I had to constantly call the police. They even set the house on fire," she said. "The people in the neighborhood had gotten a petition to get us out. It was all whites out there." The Dewittys moved for the sake of the peace and safety of their family.

Dewitty reads to her class. *Photograph courtesy of the Seattle Public Schools' archives.*

Dewitty not only broke the color barrier in teaching, but she also broke another barrier. Dewitty was a married mother. Before the war, women teachers were not allowed to be married. There were various reasons given for not wanting married teachers. It was assumed that married women didn't need the money and that they needed to be home. With the hiring of Dewitty and others, the school board's ban on hiring married women as teachers was eliminated in 1947.

In addition to her teaching, Dewitty worked tirelessly for her community. She worked for the NAACP and served as president in the 1950s. "At the time, quite a few people were afraid to belong to the NAACP....So many people were saying they were communist," she said in her oral history story. "Many Blacks were losing their jobs."

Dewitty was also a member of the Urban League and a delegate to three Democratic National Conventions. She was also appointed to the State Board Against Discrimination.

Dewitty retired from teaching in 1973. The pioneering educator passed away on August 19, 1976, at the age of sixty-three.

After Dewitty broke the color barrier, other Black women hires soon followed. Marita Johnson was hired at Edison Technical School. Peggy Johnson, who received her graduate degree from Hampton University in Virginia, was hired the next year and worked for the Seattle School Board until her retirement thirty-six years later.

8

WILLETTA RIDDLE GAYTON

The Seattle School Board's First Black Librarian

Willetta Gayton was hired in 1947 as Seattle Public Schools' first Black professional librarian. Her father-in-law, John Gayton, was one of Seattle's earliest Black pioneers.

Willetta Riddle Gayton became the first Black professional librarian hired by the Seattle Public School Board. It was a fitting profession for someone who loved to read.

Gayton's father worked for the Puget Sound Traction Light and Power building. A Boston company owned the building, and interns who lived in the building would leave newspapers out from out of town. Gayton retrieved those papers and read them from cover to cover. "I grew up reading the *New York Times*, the *Boston Tribune*, the *Bellingham Herald* and many other newspapers," she told Esther Mumford in her oral history story for the Legacy History Project. "Even though I studied geography in school, I gained more knowledge by reading those papers." She loved reading the arts and music sections of the paper. She learned of famous Black people, like Langston Hughes and Paul Robeson, who were doing great and exciting things with their lives. "Sometimes, it amazed the music teachers that I knew so much about music."

Gayton was born on August 7, 1909. Her parents, William and Salome Riddle, were some of the earliest settlers in Whatcom County. Her parents were from Yankton, Dakota Territory, and were married in 1907. Many Black people of that time had heard about and were fascinated by the

The Puget Sound Traction, Light and Power building. *Photographer, J. W. Sandison; courtesy the Whatcom Museum.*

freedom of the great western territory. Her parents packed up their belongings and moved to Nooksack, Washington. Her father had dreamed of becoming a farmer. Gayton fondly remembered in her oral history how wonderful the Natives were to her family, often bringing them smoked fish and salmon.

The family's farm life did not work out—their work didn't produce any harvest. The family gave up on farming and moved to Bellingham, Washington, where Gayton's father worked as a janitor for the Puget Sound Traction, Light and Power building. Her family lived in one of the apartments in the building. Some people who worked in the building had lived on the East Coast—that's why so many eastern newspapers were available. Gayton's mother worked at a department store as a clothes marker.

Gayton attended Fairhaven High School and was an excellent student. She loved the arts, especially ballet. Gayton's parents promised her ballet lessons, and the young Gayton was very excited when she joined a ballet class. However, in her oral history story, she explained that some of the parents of the other students objected to having a Black student in class and threatened to pull their kids from the class if she was allowed to stay. "The teacher ended up giving me private lessons." A similar incident happened when Gayton wanted to take swimming lessons at the YWCA. Parents again didn't want their children swimming with a Black girl. The teacher insisted that Gayton stay in her class.

There were very few Black people in Bellingham during that time, and Gayton loved any opportunity to visit Seattle. Since her father worked for the Puget Sound Company, she had free passes on the bus line. It was exciting for her to be around young Black people, and she eventually wanted to move there. "I had made good friends in Seattle," she said in her oral history.

Gayton graduated from Fairhaven High School in 1929. She wanted to attend the University of Washington (UW) right away, but her family's plans to move to Seattle fell through, derailing her plans. Instead, Gayton attended the Washington State Normal School, where she took teaching courses. After finishing the course, Gayton and her family moved to Seattle. For the first time in her life, Gayton was surrounded by vibrant, intelligent Black people. Gayton still wanted to attend the University of Washington, so she took a series of jobs to save money for tuition. One of those jobs was at the Phyllis Wheatley branch of the YWCA, where she worked from 1937 to 1943 as a girls' reserve secretary. "There was so much to do, and so many people needed help," she said in her oral history story. "It was almost the citadel at the wartime because of the influx of the servicemen. The Y helped with housing, especially with the girls in the war and defense plants. It was an interesting period," moving to Seattle during the war. Many communities and social clubs were formed to help with the transition of many Black Americans.

While working at the YWCA, Gayton attended the UW part time, earning her bachelor's degree in 1939.

In 1942, Willetta Riddle married James Gayton. He was the son of John T. Gayton, one of the premier Black families in the United States and one of Seattle's first Black residents. Gayton, the son of a formerly enslaved person, was appointed in August 1933 by President Franklin Roosevelt as U.S. district librarian. He remained in this position until he retired. James and Willetta Gayton adopted a daughter, Susan.

Gayton said she was the first Black person to be employed at the University of Washington. "I worked in the library part time. I liked the job, and I liked the atmosphere. After that, I decided to go back to school," she said. She received her bachelor's degree from the School of

9

LETITIA GRAVES

The First President of the Seattle Branch of the NAACP

The Seattle NAACP was founded in 1913, and Letitia Graves was the organization's first president. She was an influential leader and led many protests, including one against the movie The Birth of a Nation, *which was released in 1915.*

On April 11, 1913, President Woodrow Wilson went back on his promise to give Black Americans an "absolute fair deal." Instead, after the election, he immediately took steps to resegregate federal employees based on race.

Seattle resident Letitia Graves was so enraged at the president's reinstating of segregation that she gathered a group of other Seattle residents and formed the Seattle Branch of the National Association for the Advancement of Colored People on October 23, 1913.

Letitia Dennie Graves was born in 1863 in Illinois. She and her husband, John Henry Graves, were early settlers of Seattle, moving there around 1884.

The plan President Wilson had to resegregate federal employees was a significant setback for civil rights advocates. The policy instituted separate workspaces, bathrooms and lunchrooms, wiping out everything civil workers had fought hard to gain. Wilson explained away the reinstituted segregation by saying, "The move was not against the negroes....We are rendering them safer in their possession of the office and less likely to be discriminated against."

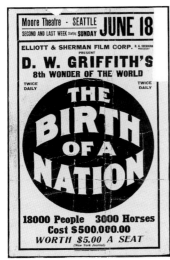

Top: Graves was the first president of the Seattle chapter of the NAACP, founded in 1913. *Public domain.*

Bottom: Graves led protests against the movie *The Birth of a Nation*. She was appalled by the depictions of Black Americans. *Photograph courtesy of the Library of Congress.*

Graves gathered a group that was virtually a who's who of prominent Black individuals in Seattle, totaling twenty-two people, and formed the Seattle branch of the NAACP. With Graves as president, the Seattle chapter was officially founded on October 13, 1913, and according to its website, this made it the first national civil rights organization in the city. The Seattle branch started just four years after the national organization was founded in New York in 1909.

Graves was a beautician, and her husband was a stonemason. She had become one of Seattle's leading citizens. In 1906, she, along with other prominent women of the time, such as Susie Revels Cayton, organized the Dorcas Charity Club. Seattle's Children Home needed help finding a home for Black twin girls who had rickets. The club was formed in response to the request from the children's hospital. The women of the Dorcas Club arranged for the twins to be placed in a foster home and supported them until they were adopted.

Graves was a passionate and tireless fighter and supporter of the dignity of Black Americans. In 1915, the film *Birth of a Nation*, from D.W. Griffith, was released. The film was a commercial success, with the theme of life after the Civil War. The members of the Klu Klux Klan were depicted as heroes who saved the South from marauding Black killers and rapists. The film was scheduled to be shown in Seattle. After learning of the film's degradation of Black Americans, Graves and the NAACP protested the film's showing in Seattle. However, the film was wildly successful during its initial run, and despite her efforts, the film premiered as scheduled.

A large number of Black people, many of them from the South, moved to Seattle in the early days to escape the horrors of lynchings and discrimination experienced in other parts of the country. While Seattle did not have the overt animus, discrimination still followed Black Americans. Under Graves's leadership, the NAACP fought and protested for Black Americans in housing, education and employment. The NAACP also organized and celebrated Emancipation Day, a day to commemorate the emancipation of the enslaved.

Letitia Graves died on September 16, 1952, at the age of eighty-nine. She left behind a legacy of unparallel social and political activism.

10

MADAME LUELLA RUTH BROWN BOYER (BRENT)

Everett's First Black Woman Business Owner

Madame Luella Ruth Brown Boyer (Brent) was Everett's first Black woman to become a business owner. She owned a hair and beauty salon and worked as a makeup artist at the Everett Theater.

When Luella Ruth Brown Boyer (Brent) was growing up, her parents had great expectations for her and her brother, Samuel. However, during the early 1900s, roles were clearly defined for women in general and Black women in particular. Luella's career choices were usually confined to being a domestic servant. A Black woman owning her own business was an unlikely dream. But Luella was a unique woman with a boldly independent streak. That independent spirit led her to become the first Black woman to own a business in the city of Everett. She opened the Ladies Hair Emporium in 1902, and it turned into a very successful business. An article in the *Seattle Republican*, the largest Black-owned and -operated paper in the state, said, "The leading society ladies of Everett patronize her, and on the whole, [she] has built up a most excellent business." It should be noted that her salon served both white and Black customers—a necessity, since the Black population of Everett at the time was minuscule.

Luella Brown was born in 1868 in Keosauqua, Iowa. Her parents, Lewis and Elizabeth Brown, had migrated from Missouri to Iowa around 1864. According to the Everett Public Library historian, her father was a descendant of the original enslaved people who were sold in Jamestown,

Virginia, in 1619. To escape the horrors of the remnants of slavery, her parents moved to Iowa, a free state. Her father worked as a laborer, and her mother worked as a maid. Her parents wanted Luella and Samuel to have an education and to live better lives. Her younger brother, Samuel Brown (1875–1950), became a lawyer and had a long and notable career as a civil rights lawyer. He also founded the first NAACP chapter in Des Moines, Iowa.

Luella Brown met her husband, John Boyer, in Iowa, and they were married on May 20, 1896 (or 1897). She was around twenty-eight years old, and he was twenty-five years older than her. Boyer was born in 1844 in Pennsylvania. He worked as a barber and as a traveling salesman, selling hair-care products.

In 1902, the couple moved to Everett, Washington, seeking better opportunities and a new life. Unfortunately, shortly after moving to Everett, their marriage broke up, and John left. Luella Boyer was left to fend for herself and their daughter, Esther Marie, whom they had adopted. Being a single mother in the early 1900s could not have been an easy task for the young woman. She declared herself a widow, a more acceptable title for a woman during the early 1900s. Her shop was located at 2928 Colby Avenue. She rebranded herself as Madame Luella Boyer. According to historians, many Black women in the hair-care industry used the madame's title. Madame Luella Boyer was a hairdresser and sold a line of hair-care products. Through the years, she expanded her business to include dermatology services. Most historians are unsure what the dermatology services were, but perhaps it included a line of skincare products.

In real estate, the phrase goes, "Location, location, location." Boyer's shop was situated in the heart of the theater district. The theater district was a thriving community filled with businesses, people and shops and was the perfect location.

Madame Boyer worked at the Everett Theater as a janitor, making one dollar a night when she first started. She was perhaps a makeup artist and hairstylist for some of the performers at the theater, particularly the Black performers. In all likelihood, she did the makeup for the performers in the musical *In Dahomey*, which featured vaudevillians Bert Williams and George Walker. *In Dahomey* was one of the first hit musicals performed and written entirely by Black people that was performed on major theatrical stages. The musical was a national and an international hit, playing to acclaim on stages from New York to London. The troupe performed at the Everett Theater on January 16, 1905.

The Everett Museum was a showcase for talented musicians, and Madame Luella often worked as a makeup artist for some actors. *Photogrpah courtesy of the Everett Public Library.*

Inside the Everett Museum. When Madame Boyer first started her business, she worked as a janitor at the museum to make ends meet. *Photograph courtesy of the Everett Historical Museum.*

Madame Boyer's salon on Colby Avenue still stands in Everett. It is now a nail salon. *Photograph by Lisa Labovitch; courtesy of the Everett Public Library.*

On April 20, 1910, Boyer remarried Bertrand Brent, a white man from Missouri who worked as a janitor for the Seattle Public Library and as a waiter. He was born on May 20, 1877, and died in Edmonds on March 25, 1957.

The couple settled into a loving and prosperous life. They entered the real estate market and amassed several properties and houses in both Snohomish and King County.

Madame Luella Brown Boyer Brent continued to thrive, meeting her parents' expectations. Like her brother, she was socially and politically active. She participated in and spoke at forums on various topics, including those of racial and gender inequality. She wrote articles for the *Seattle Republican*. In one article, she is quoted as saying, "Victory shall be ours if we adhere to the principles of unity, peace, and harmony."

Unfortunately, her life was tragically cut short. Madame Luella Ruth Brown Boyer (Brent) died on December 18, 1912, from complications of diabetes.

11

BREAKING THE COLOR LINE

Boeing Hires Black Rosie the Riveters

During World War II, Boeing and other aircraft companies hired a wave of Black women who worked toward the war effort. These women were known as Rosie the Riveters. Three Black Rosies shared their personal experiences of being among the first Black employees at the Boeing Company.

It may be hard to imagine the Boeing Company ever having a racial exclusion policy, but the company did. But after a hard-fought, three-year-long civil rights battle, in January 1942, Florise Spearman was hired as the first Black employee at Boeing. She was hired as a stenographer. A few months later, in April 1942, Dorothy West Williams became the first Black person hired as a production worker.

When World War II began, Boeing played a pivotal role in the war effort. Many Black Americans migrated to Seattle looking for jobs in the war-effort industries. There was only one problem: the largest employer in the city had a policy against hiring Black people or any nonwhite people for that matter.

Even though Boeing needed every hand to keep up with the demand for planes, the company still didn't hire any Black people. In 1939, Hutchen R. Hutchins, a civil rights activist, a member of the Communist Party and a reporter for the *Northwest Enterprise* (a Black newspaper), organized a broad coalition of activists, community leaders, civil rights groups and church leaders to pressure Boeing to reverse its racial exclusion policy. According to "Battle at Boeing," an article for the Seattle Civil Rights and Labor History Project at the University of Washington, this was the first flexing of the small but strong Black community. Boeing blamed its union, the International

Black women riveters were hired at various companies and worked toward the war effort. Pictured are the women who worked at the Buick Plant in 1942. *Photograph courtesy of the National Archives.*

Association of Machinists (IAM), citing its stance against allowing nonwhite members into the union.

According to the Center for the Study of the Pacific Northwest, the Black population in Seattle rose from 400 in 1900 to 3,800 in 1940. If Black Americans moved to Seattle expecting a utopia, they were greatly disappointed.

The Boeing Company was founded in 1916. Until World War II, it had not hired any Black people, even though President Franklin D. Roosevelt (in June 1941) issued Executive Order 8802, which prohibited companies with government contracts from practicing racial discrimination in hiring.

Boeing's refusal to hire Black employees had become a broadening concern. Supreme Court Justice Thurgood Marshall, a lawyer for the NAACP, persuaded the Seattle branch to pressure the company. The NAACP filed a complaint against the company to the Fair Employment Practice Committee. With mounting pressure and the demand for more workers because of the war's demands, Boeing finally relented and, in 1942, hired its first Black American.

Perspectives on Working at Boeing

During World War II, more than 500,000 Black Rosies worked in war-effort industries, such as at the Boeing Company and the shipyard. The Museum of History and Industry conducted oral histories with Rosies for its Rosie the Riveter Project. Rosie the Riveter was an iconic depiction of a female factory worker flexing her muscles, encouraging other women to join the World War II effort with the declaration: "We Can Do It." Profiled in the following sections are three Black Rosies among the first wave of Black workers hired by Boeing in 1943. They shared their perspectives on working for Boeing in the early years.

Katie R. Burks

Katie R. Burks grew up in Birmingham, Alabama, and always had a desire to travel. When World War II started, the U.S. government needed people to help with the war effort, including working at airplane factories. "I wanted to come to Seattle because I wanted to travel, and we figured Seattle was the farthest place we could go," said Burks in her oral history interview with Anita Warmflash for MOHAI's Rosies the Riveter Project. She described her experience as one in the first waves of Black women working for Boeing. When Burks was eighteen years old in Birmingham, she attended a training program through a New Deal program under President Franklin Roosevelt. She went to an unemployment agency and learned that the government needed people to work at Boeing to help make airplanes for the war effort.

Burks said she was excited at the prospect of moving across the country to a new and exciting place. She and her sister, four other girls and two boys traveled four nights and five days by train from Birmingham to Seattle. Her parents initially objected to the sisters traveling so far away but relented and were proud that their girls were so bold.

In 1943, Burks said that when they arrived in Seattle, they moved into a dormitory in Georgetown until they found their own place. "Because we were so young, they had people looking out for us," she said. They had curfews, and there were plenty of recreational activities.

Once the sisters reported for work at Boeing, they went through training and received their job assignments. "They put me in mechanics, and I found it very interesting," said Burks. "I drilled holes, measured and put parts together."

Burks said they worked long hours, usually around ten to twelve hours a day. She noted that the section of the plane she worked on was dependent on what was going on with the war.

During her entire career at Boeing, Burks worked as a mechanic. "I enjoyed it. Even after coming back after the war, I still wanted to work as a mechanic," she said.

Even though Boeing had been slow and even defiant in hiring Black Americans, Burks described her time there as a wonderful experience. "Everyone from my shop was from a different state, and I enjoyed getting to know and talking to everyone, especially this woman from Germany. She was very interesting, and I learned a lot from her," said Burks.

As for the work environment, Burks said she primarily worked with women because most men were serving in the war. "I think because I was so young, most of the people were nice to me, and I think everyone just wanted to work together to get the planes out. I was a fast worker, so I think they liked my work," said Burks.

Burks said one negative at work was that the Black workers weren't allowed to join the workers' union, but they had to have a permit. The permits cost $3.00 per month. Union dues were $1.50 per month, and the white women were permitted to join the union. Burks said many restaurants around town initially did not want the Black workers at their establishments. "We didn't care all that much because we loved going to Canada when we had time off," she said.

There was another incident that stood out in Burks's mind because it was so rare. "When the company hired boys from high school to work part time, some of them were really nasty and called us dirty names. I would stand up for myself and reported them to the supervisor, and they were let go," said Burks.

Burks emphasized that she always had great supervisors while working at Boeing. As long as she did her work, the supervisors had no problem with her and often protected Black workers from bad situations.

Burks, her sister and two other girls who moved to Seattle together decided to stay together. They rented a house together and settled into their new life at Boeing and in Seattle. They joined the Phyllis Wheatley branch of the YWCA, which provided most of their social life. "It was nice—we were a part of the social club at the YWCA," said Burks. "We would invite service guys to the functions." They also attended United Service Organization (USO) functions, where they danced with the young servicemen. "We had plenty of chaperones," she said. The USO is a charitable organization that supports the U.S. military. It provides live entertainment and, in years past, sponsored dances and social functions for the troops.

Burks said one of Boeing's and Seattle's best aspects as a young woman in the 1940s was the independence they provided her. "We worked the second shift, and the hours were 4:30 to 12:30. We usually went to the movies after work because there was a movie theater that stayed open all night," she said.

However, there were some things she had to get used to while working and living in Seattle in those early years. "In the South, you knew where to go and what was accepted—here, you didn't know. There were no signs that said 'Whites Only' or anything like that. You just had to do a trial-and-error thing," said Burks.

As time went on, Burks felt very welcomed in Seattle in most aspects. She said her landlord was like a mother to her. She joined the Peoples Institutional Baptist Church, where she was treated like family. "I still got homesick, especially on Sundays, because that was a family day at home. We did a lot of letter writing," she said.

After the war, in 1945, the Boeing plant was closed. Out of a job, Burks went to work folding laundry. In 1946, she married Carl Burks, her childhood sweetheart, who had moved to Seattle after serving in the military. She and her husband had one son. They were happily married for fifty years until Carl's death in 1997.

In 1950, Burks heard that Boeing was hiring again, so she applied and was hired back. Burks did not realize that she and the other Black workers were making history by breaking the color barrier. But what she cherished most about the experience was the lifelong friendships she made with the women she traveled with from Alabama to Seattle.

She worked again as a mechanic and remained at Boeing until her retirement in 1991. And yes, she did indulge her traveling spirit—the spirit that brought her out to Seattle. "I've traveled to Rome. I traveled to the Caribbean. I've traveled to many places. About three times a year, we went somewhere," Burks said.

Burks said she really loved her time at Boeing and loved being a mechanic. She said if she had done anything differently, she would have gone to college. "A lot of my friends went to the University of Washington, but I would have still worked as a mechanic. When I'm on a plane, I can always look and see the work I did when working there," Burks said with pride.

Burks, reflecting on her time at Boeing in the early and later years, said she was always treated fairly and even kindly by her supervisors. Boeing even featured her in a documentary it produced featuring people in different

During World War II, Boeing and other aircraft companies hired a wave of Black women who worked toward the war effort. The women were known as "Rosie the Riveters." *Photograph courtesy of the Library of Congress.*

aspects of their lives. They focused on her life in retirement. "They followed me to church, shopping, at home. They had pictures of me working at Boeing. The documentary aired on channel 11," explained Burks.

Mrs. Burks died in January 2021.

VIVIAN LAYNE: AN ORAL HISTORY FROM THE ROSIE THE RIVETER PROJECT

Vivian Layne was born and raised in Birmingham, Alabama, and joined her sister Katie Burks in a life-changing decision. Along with four other girls and two boys, the women boarded a train to Seattle, Washington, to work for the Boeing Company to support the war effort. It was 1943, and she had graduated from high school; Layne had plans to attend college to study nursing. "I'm glad I made that decision. I've never regretted it," she said in her oral history interview with Anita Warmflash from the Museum of Industry and History for its Rosie the Riveter Project.

She was excited about the opportunity to make parts for planes. "We took the train to Seattle, and it was a long train ride. It lasted five days and four nights," she said.

Layne said she was confident about how she, her sister and the four other girls would fare in Seattle because of their upbringing. "Our mothers had taught us right from wrong and things we should or shouldn't do," she said.

Layne explained that when they arrived in Seattle, dormitory housing was provided. They all had chores while living there. Eventually, the six girls who traveled to Seattle decided to stick together and rented a small house. "We had a sweet landlady who treated us like her daughters."

Layne explained that Boeing made sure they worked in a safe environment, and the supervisors were nice and even spoke up for the Black workers when warranted. She worked as a mechanic in the chemical dye division for her first assignment. "The apron I had to wear was so heavy I could hardly move. I explained the problem to my supervisor, and she was very understanding and nice about it," she said. She was transferred to a different area, where she had to measure parts, so she had to undergo training again. "I went to school, and I worked. I didn't mind because I loved taking courses, and I was a quick learner," she said.

Layne received a promotion to hydraulic panels and finally to assembly. That's where she experienced prejudice. "There was a group of people from Montana who worked in that area. They didn't want to work with me because I was Black," she said. Their attitudes didn't bother Layne; she said she was there to do a job. However, she drew the line when those coworkers became verbally abusive. "They would say to me that I had a tail and that all Black people had tails," she said. "I will never forget what the supervisor, Josephine Ryan, said, 'You're not talking to that girl like that; I have a daughter about her age.'" Layne said Ryan was very forceful. "They

Rosie the Riveters became essential workers in the war effort during World War II. Pictured is a riveter at Lockheed Aircraft in California. *Photograph courtesy of the National Archives.*

never bothered me again. It wasn't a shock to me, but I wasn't bothered because I always knew I was a person."

Layne said she loved her job at Boeing and that she had many great supervisors who didn't let the Black workers get abused verbally and certainly not physically.

In 1945, after the war had ended, Boeing was shut down. Layne said she was not surprised and was happy that the boys were returning from the war.

Layne was called back to work in 1950, when the plant reopened, but she decided not to return. She worked for a hotel and at the shipyard in the interim and eventually embarked on a new career at the University of Washington. "I worked in the lab, at first with animals and then working with doctors in the biochemistry department," she said.

Layne had fond memories as one in the first waves of Black Rosie the Riveters.

KATHERINE D. THOMPKINS

Katherine Thompkins heard about the Boeing Company hiring women to work in airplane manufacturing while living in Tulsa, Oklahoma. "I was just out of high school, and I needed a job," she told Anita Warmflash from the Museum of History and Industry for its Rosie the Riveter Project. She had been training at a school for welding through the National Youth Administration Program that had been instituted by President Franklin Roosevelt. "I was willing to train for any job," she said. "I looked on the map and found that Seattle was the farthest from Oklahoma. That sounded good to me."

Thompkins boarded a train from Tulsa to Seattle in 1943 to begin a new life in a new place, surrounded by new people. "I left my mother and sister in Oklahoma. My mother was really proud I was taking this step," she said.

Thompkins wanted the job at Boeing to save up enough money to help her mother, who was ill. "I was hoping to send my mother to the Mayo Clinic," she said. Her mother, unfortunately, passed away in 1948.

Like most riveters, when Thompkins arrived in Seattle, she lived in a dormitory on East Marginal Way and Carlson Avenue. It was short-term housing, lasting about a month. After that, she moved to more permanent housing.

Reporting to work, the first thing she noticed was that the workforce was made up primarily of women. "There were very few men, and there were few African Americans," she said. Most men were off fighting the war, and Boeing had only recently begun hiring Black people. She was part of the first group of hires.

Thompkins had been trained as a welder, but the company placed her in another department. "I was trained in sheet metal and riveting. I worked as a mechanic," she said.

Thompkins said she was happy with her work and was given good opportunities. "I worked at the Little Red Barn as a mechanic, drilling holes in the wing of the plane," she said. She then transferred to Plant II, where she worked as a forklift driver. "Luckily, I could drive. I really liked working the forklift," she said. "I drove all over the plant, and it was fun."

Thompkins then started riveting parts. "I did that for years. I developed different skills. That's the thing about our generation—we did what we had to do to survive, and we made the best of it," she said.

Thompkins was proud of the work she did at Boeing. She explained a lot of preparation had to be done before the actual riveting took place. Part of her job was to cut the parts for the plane.

"Building a plane then was not like it is today. It was like making a cake; during World War II, you started from scratch," she said.

Thompkins said Boeing was a responsible company that made sure to practice safety measures—things like making sure everyone was fitted with the proper googles and steel-toed shoes. As far as working there, Thompkins said, "It was fair in a way, and you had problems in a way—like it is now." One of the problems she pointed out was that Black workers had to do more of the menial work. "After the riveting, the area needed to be cleaned. I usually had to relinquish my job to do the clean-up. One of the white ladies would come over and do my job while I cleaned the plane or the floor," she explained. Another issue for Thompkins was that Black workers could not join the union. However, Black workers needed permits that cost twice as much as union dues. As time went on, Thompkins said some Black workers tried to form an all-Black union, but that never took off.

Thompkins said there were few days off while working at Boeing. When they did have time off, she and her friends would go to functions where young women were invited to meet soldiers. She met her husband at one of those functions.

After V-J Day, the plant closed in about nine months. "They never told us that after the war ended, we wouldn't have jobs," she said. (V-J Day was the day the Allies won victory over Japan. It was August 15, 1945, when Japan surrendered.)

Unfortunately, Thompkins's husband became sick and received an honorable discharge from service. He had contracted tuberculosis and died. Thompkins was convinced that the military knew he was sick before he was discharged. She had children to care for and got a job at a nursing home when she lost her job at Boeing. When she heard that Boeing was hiring again, she applied and was rehired.

Thompkins loved living in Seattle and became very involved in her community. She joined the NAACP, and she joined Mount Zion Baptist Church, which, today, has the largest Black congregation in Washington State.

12

JENNIE SAMUELS

Pioneering Clubwoman

Jennie Samuels was the second president of the Washington State Federation of Colored Women's Clubs. She hosted the 1924 convention, which attracted more than two hundred women. Her first act as president was to establish a scholarship for Black children who wanted to pursue higher education.

The history of the Black club dates to the days of slavery. Black women have traditionally come together to work to improve the lives of Black Americans. Jennie Samuels was the quintessential clubwoman. The Everett, Washington resident worked tirelessly, helping and guiding women who were navigating their way to better lives. She served as president of the Washington Association of Colored Women's Clubs (WACWC) for four years. During her time as president, the club had more than two thousand members statewide and is still active.

Before her work with the WACWC, she founded the Nannie Burroughs Study Club. Samuels was an ardent admirer of Burroughs, an educator, writer, activist, suffragist and advocate for Black people. Burroughs founded the Woman's Industrial Club of Louisville, Kentucky. She addressed the needs of Black women and coached them on improving their lives. She encouraged and taught women to enhance their skills, whether in professions, such as bookkeeping, millinery or clerical work, or in nonprofessional work, such as cooking, sewing and laundry work.

Samuels embraced these ideals, and like Burroughs, she led women in improving their lives spiritually, socially, professionally and politically.

Thank our God that we have something to do, whether we like it or not. Doing our duty brings out the best that is in us and will breed in us a self control, strength of will, cheerfulness and content and a score of virtues which idleness fails to give.

MRS. J. B. SAMUELS,
President at the publishing of this book.

Year, 1922-1923.

Jennie Samuels was the president of the Washington State Federation of Colored Women's Clubs and hosted the national convention in Everett in 1924. *Photograph courtesy of the University of Washington's special collections 1081-002 box 1, folder 11, Nettie J. Asberry Papers.*

In 1920, Samuels welcomed women from across the state to Everett High School, where the Washington Association of Colored Women's Clubs held its convention. It was a busy convention full of events and exhibits, according to the *Everett Herald*. Dignitaries included Roland Hartley, who had served as the mayor of Everett, became a member of the Washington State House of Representatives and eventually was elected governor of the state. Items on the agenda included a discussion of the life of Frederick Douglass, the plight of the elderly, the welfare of children and the fight for equality. There were also pieces of artwork and crafts displayed in the school's basement. The *Everett Herald* described the art as "excellent workmanship."

Samuels believed that clubwomen had the strength and talent to make a difference in the world. In a cookbook published by the WACWC, she is quoted as saying, "Thank God that we have something to do, whether we like it or not. Doing our duty brings out the best that is in us and will breed in us self-control, the strength of will, cheerfulness and content, and a score of virtues which idleness fails to give."

Jennie Samuels was born on October 1, 1868, in Salem, North Carolina, as Jennie B. Phelps. In 1890, she married John B. Samuels, a laborer from Louisville, Kentucky.

Samuels's son was John Wesley Samuels. Pictured is his senior portrait from Everett High School, circa 1912. *Courtesy of the Everett Public Library.*

The couple moved to Saint Paul, Minnesota, where their son, John Wesley Samuels, was born in 1891. As with many Black couples, the Samuelses were looking for a better life when they moved out west to Everett, Washington, circa 1897. John Samuels worked as a custodian to provide for his family. John Wesley graduated from Everett High School in 1912. He enlisted and served in the army during World War I and achieved the rank of battalion sergeant major. He received an honorable discharge and returned to Everett, where he worked as a secretary for the American Boiler and Iron Works.

Jennie Samuels was a housewife who immersed herself in clubwoman activities. In her speech at the 1924 convention, according to the *Everett Herald*, she spoke eloquently about the need for advocacy. "It is our duty, as representatives of the colored people of the state, to do all in our power to assume our true position in the life of the nation and to break down a barrier of misunderstanding of the colored people," she said. "In this work, our churches and clubs should take an active part."

The Samuelses' home was a hub of activity. They hosted many functions, including club meetings. Their home was listed in *The Negro Motorist Green Book*, a travel guide for Black American motorists published from 1936 to 1967. Because many hotels, restaurants, salons and other businesses refused service to Black people, the book listed safe places to stay and places to buy services and products when traveling.

Jennie Samuels was an admirer of Nannie Burroughs (1883–1961). She was the founder and president of the Nannie Burroughs Study Club. Burroughs was a Black American educator, suffragist, writer and activist for racial and gender equality. She founded the National Training School for Women and Girls in Washington, D.C. Burroughs also wrote a twelve-point manifesto titled "12 Things the Negro Must Do for Himself":

1. *The negro must learn to put first things first. The first things are education, development of character traits, a trade and homeownership.*
2. *The negro must stop expecting God and white folks to do for him what he can do for himself.*
3. *The negro must keep himself, his children and his home clean and make the surroundings in which he lives comfortable and attractive.*
4. *The negro must dress more appropriately for work and for leisure.*
5. *The negro must make his religion an everyday practice and not just a Sunday go-to-meeting emotional affair.*
6. *The negro must highly resolve to wipe out mass ignorance.*
7. *The negro must stop charging his failures up to his "color."*
8. *The negro must overcome his bad habits.*
9. *He must improve his conduct in public places.*
10. *The negro must learn how to operate businesses for people.*
11. *The average so-called educated negro will have to come down out of the air. He is too inflated over nothing.*
12. *The negro must stop forgetting his friends, "Remember."*

Inset: Samuels was greatly influenced by Nannie Burroughs, a Black educator, civil rights activist and businesswoman. *Courtesy of the Library of Congress.*

Above: Samuels hosted one of the largest conventions during the Washington Association of Colored Women's Clubs era. *Courtesy of Washington Association of Colored Women's Clubs.*

The Samuelses' family home on Wetmore Avenue. *Photographer, Lisa Labovitch; courtesy of the Everett Public Library.*

Jennie Samuels passed away on August 13, 1948, at her home after a prolonged illness. Her son, John Wesley, died six years later at a veterans' hospital in Vancouver, Washington. Her husband, James, died seven months later at an Everett hospital. The couple had been married for fifty-eight years.

Jennie Samuels was a woman committed to her faith and club life throughout her adult life. She continually fought to improve the lives of Black Americans. "Faith, trust, push and stability are essential to our cultural and social growth," Samuels said in her speech at the WACWC in 1924. She lived her life by that philosophy.

13

NORA B. ADAMS

The Seattle School Board's First Black Woman Principal

Nora B. Adams was hired as the principal of T.T. Minor Elementary School in 1970, making her the first Black woman principal employed by the Seattle Public School Board.

Nora B. Adams spent thirty-seven years of her life dedicated to education. In 1970, she became the first Black woman principal hired by the Seattle Public School Board.

Adams was born on November 20, 1928, in a segregated town, Terrell, Texas. Education was a vital component of her upbringing. She grew up in a family of educators who stressed the importance of education. Her father, J.W. Long, was the principal of a Black elementary school that Adams attended. Her mother was Nadie Johnson Long. She was the youngest of six children.

As a child, Adams had many interests and talents. She took piano lessons and played a variety of genres, from jazz to classical. Her parents wanted their daughter to have a better education than her hometown could offer, so she moved to Dallas at the urging of her older brother Wendell, a teacher in Dallas. Like her family predicted, it was an excellent educational experience, and Adams graduated from Booker T. Washington High School in 1945 and quickly transitioned to college. She attended Bishop College for one year before she decided she wanted a different path. During World War II, three of her sisters moved to Seattle. Adams followed in 1946 and enrolled at the University of Washington, where she

Right: Nora B. Adams was hired as the principal of T.T. Minor Elementary School in 1970. *Courtesy of the Seattle Public Schools Archives.*

Below: Nora Adams, principal, and her staff of Seward Elementary School. *Courtesy of the Seattle Public Schools Archives.*

MRS. NORA ADAMS - PRINCIPAL
ROW 3: JOHN RUNDBERG, ANN ROTERMUND, SIDNEY GILL-ERICKSON, DENNIS SOLDAT, GEIR ROSVIK, BERNICE MOORE, VALERIYE LEWIS
ROW 2: REBECCA MC CULLOUGH, JOY MENKE, MARILYN JAEGER, DARLEEN DAMON, LINDA HARVELAND, GARY GLOCKNER
ROW 1: PENNY MELTON, NORA ADAMS, NANCY INGLE, CAROLE LYNCH, KAROLYN BACKHOLM, ROSE MARIE SILLENCE

earned her bachelor's degree in education in 1952 and a master's degree in education in 1959. Adams began her teaching career at Sharples Junior High School. After a year, she began teaching at T.T. Minor Elementary School. She taught there for seven years before moving to New Jersey, where she taught until she was promoted to become principal of schools in Lawnside, Magnolia and Camden, New Jersey.

Adams returned to Seattle in 1970 to accept the job of principal of T.T. Minor Elementary School. The 1970s were a contentious time in Seattle and the rest of the country due to the segregation of schools. Adams was appointed to the district's desegregation committee.

Even though the U.S. Supreme Court had ruled in the landmark school desegregation case *Brown v. The Board of Education* in 1954 and declared that segregated schools were unconstitutional, school boards across the country had been slow to desegregate. Years of redlining in housing had created a racial divide in the school system. There was no separate but equal, and civil rights groups wanted action. There were lawsuits brought forth by the NAACP. The school board had tried various methods to desegregate, such as creating magnet schools. Students were allowed to switch schools outside of their neighborhoods voluntarily. But that compromise did little to bridge the segregation gap. Weary of the ongoing segregation, in 1966, civil rights groups organized a boycott of schools. Between March 31 and April 1, thousands of students in the central district boycotted Seattle schools. Not wanting future boycotts or lawsuits, the Seattle School Board developed a plan. In 1970, the desegregation plan involved having more than two thousand middle school students bused to schools in different neighborhoods. The plan was controversial, to say the least. It was hailed as a significant blow against segregation by some civil rights leaders and decried by antibusing groups, such as Citizens Against Mandatory Busing. By 1977, the plan was expanded to include all school grades. Busing in the Seattle School System ended on November 20, 1996, and students were given the option of returning to their neighborhood schools.

Adams was married to A.J. Crawley in 1948, and they had a son, Alonzo Crawley. In 1971, she married Robert Adams.

Adams continued to serve as principal to Bryant, Sacagawea, Dunlap and Seward Elementary Schools. She retired in 1989 and unfortunately passed away in 2004.

In Adams's obituary in the *Seattle Times*, her sister Mildred McHenry explained what a beloved principal she was. She said she found many letters from students thanking her for her work and guidance. Adams was also a member of Trinity Parish Episcopal Church, where she sang in the choir and served on the board of directors. Reverend Paul Collins recalled that "she was always so full of energy—a spark plug wherever she was," he said. "She really was loved by a lot of people."

Adams has been described as a woman who embraced life. She traveled, played bridge, bowled

Nora Adams left more than $600,000 in her will to the Seattle Public School Scholarship Fund. *Courtesy of the Seattle Public Schools Archives.*

and enjoyed her family and friends. According to Historylink.org, her friends described her as cheerful, congenial and warm.

Adams was also a savvy investor. She left a million-dollar estate upon her death, with more than $600,000 bestowed to the Seattle Public School Scholarship Fund. The rest of the money was left to cancer and heart research.

A scholarship fund was established in 1974 to give financial assistance for college to students from Seattle Public Schools. The money goes to students from traditional and alternative high schools.

Adams left a legacy of education and a blueprint for living a well-lived life. "She was going all the time," said McHenry in the *Seattle Times* obituary. "[She] would spend time in Florida, along the Oregon Coast, reading and sketching." She told McHenry that she would keep going until "she can't go anymore."

14

DOROTHY HOLLINGSWORTH

First Black Woman Elected to the Seattle Public School Board

Dorothy Hollingsworth was disappointed when she wasn't hired as a Seattle teacher in 1949, but she later became the first Black woman elected to the Seattle School Board. She later because the first director of the Head Start Program under President Johnson.

In 1949, Dorothy Hollingsworth applied for a job as a teacher for the Seattle Public Schools. She thought she had the qualifications for the position because of her teaching experience in North Carolina. "I worked five years in teaching before I moved to Seattle, so I went to the school administration and applied," Hollingsworth said in her Seattle Civil Rights and Labor History Project oral history. "I had an interview with the personnel director, and she said, 'Well, Seattle has hired its first Negro teacher and it's [school board is] not ready to hire more.'"

Hollingsworth said that she was disappointed because she thought Seattle had a different mindset than her home state of North Carolina. "I decided not to let that turn me around. That's what I tell kids today—don't let one experience stop you or destroy you—keep going."

Hollingsworth was not deterred by the rejection and went on to achieve several firsts in her life. She became the first Black woman in Washington to serve on the school board, the first Black woman elected to the school board and the first director of the Seattle School Board's Head Start Program.

Hollingsworth was born on October 19, 1920, in Bishopville, South Carolina, and her family moved to Winston-Salem, North Carolina, when she was very young. She graduated from Paine College in Augusta,

Hollingsworth was the first Black woman to serve on the Seattle School Board. *Courtesy of the Seattle Public Schools Archives.*

Georgia, in 1941. Hollingsworth began her teaching career in South Carolina before moving to North Carolina to continue teaching. In 1946, she and her husband, Raft Hollingsworth, who had been stationed at Fort Lewis, moved to Seattle. Perhaps she and her husband thought Seattle would offer new opportunities and a place to escape the racial hatred of the South. "There wasn't as much integration as I thought it would be," explained Hollingsworth. "Housing had pockets where Blacks lived. I expected that we would all be one. I was surprised, but I wasn't overwhelmed by it. For instance, I went over to Port Orchard one day with my husband, and I went into this restaurant and asked for a Coke. The manager said, 'I could sell it to you, but you can't drink it here.' I begin to think to myself, 'You may be a long way from home, but the practice isn't much different.'"

After applying to a series of jobs, Hollingsworth said she became enlightened. When she applied at the telephone company, the interviewer noted she had a college education. "She said, 'I'll call you,'" said Hollingsworth. "I knew she wasn't going to call."

Hollingsworth landed on her feet with a job as an investigator for the State Department of Welfare. She enrolled at the University of Washington and received her master's degree in social work in 1959. Hollingsworth started working as a social worker for the Seattle Public Schools. She became a legendary advocate for the children of the district. "[Once], a child was referred to me who got into fights on the playground all the time," she explained. "I asked the teacher, 'Why is she fighting.' The teacher said, 'She fights because they call her [the N-word], and I said that's all right because that's a term of endearment in the South.'" Hollingsworth was appalled by the teacher's response. "I'm sure you upset the child; that is not a term of endearment....I talked to the principal about teachers needing some human relations courses," she said.

In the 1960s, Hollingsworth became active in the civil rights movement. She joined the NAACP, the Madison branch of the YWCA and Christian Friends of Racial Equality. Hollingsworth fought hard to eliminate covenants and redlining in housing.

She became involved with the Christian Friends of Racial Equality because of her friendship with Bertha Pitts Campbell. "It was an interracial group, and I supported them. They were trying to bring all races together to bring down barriers," she said. "One of the organization's initiatives was in the real estate market. [Members] tried to get real estate agents to sell to racial minorities." Hollingsworth recounted her own story of housing discrimination. "I went to buy a house in the Madison area. [The realtor] told me, 'I could sell it to you, but you wouldn't be able to live in it.' So, that was the kind of attitude you had to deal with."

The year 1965 proved to be a pivotal one for Hollingsworth. She was selected to head the Head Start Program, making her the first Black woman to run a city agency. Head Start was a federal program that was part of President Lyndon B. Johnson's War on Poverty. The program aided children between the ages three and five years old who were living in poverty with nutritional, health and learning services. It was a lifeline for many families. The program has served more than 39 million children. Hollingsworth successfully implemented the program according to the federal guidelines. According to Historylink.org, with her expertise, Hollingsworth was

In 1965, Hollingsworth became the first director of the Head Start Program as part of President Johnson's antipoverty program. *Courtesy of the Seattle Public Schools Archives.*

appointed to the national advisory board of *Sesame Street*, the children's television show broadcast on PBS. "I think the program had a tremendous impact," said Hollingsworth.

Hollingsworth made history in 1975, when she became the first Black woman to serve on the Seattle Public School Board, and again in 1979, when she was elected president of the board. She served a six-year term. It was also historical that the Black community felt they had a say in their children's education. It was also the first time the Seattle School Board had a female majority.

Hollingsworth's tenure on the school board came at a contentious time in the school system's history. The Seattle School System was grappling with segregation in the schools and the best avenue toward desegregation. The Seattle School System had decided to use a very controversial busing plan. Hollingsworth explained why desegregation was so important. "Some parents would say to me, 'Do you think a child would learn more because a Black child is sitting next to a white child.' I said no, but if the white child gets resources and the Black child is sitting next to him, then I expect both to get equal resources," she said. Even though busing was very controversial, other methods had failed.

Hollingsworth explained that there were seven board members, and six of the seven were committed to desegregation. "They tried to chair the desegregation committee," she said. "I didn't want it to become a racial thing, so I worked on the committee. I remember saying, 'I don't remember saying you could segregate, so don't ask me to desegregate.'"

After her tenure with the school board, Hollingsworth was elected to the State Board of Education and served from 1984 to 1993, a position that allowed her to set school policy with legislatures.

Dorothy Hollingsworth was a brilliant and compassionate educator who left a lasting legacy of putting the needs of children first.

Hollingsworth is a member of the First African Methodist Episcopal Church, the NAACP and the Delta Sigma Theta sorority. She has received many awards over the years, including the Edwin T. Pratt Award, Nordstrom's Cultural Diversity Award and the Isabel Colman Pierce Award.

15

DR. DOLORES SILAS

The First Black Woman Elected to the Tacoma City Council

Dr. Dolores Silas is a trailblazer who holds many firsts in her life, including being the first Black woman elected to the Tacoma City Council and the first Black administrator in Tacoma public schools.

On July 1, 2021, a ceremony was held to rename Woodrow Wilson High School to Dr. Dolores Silas High School. One by one, current and former students came up to the petite, impeccably dressed ninety-five-year-old to say what an honor it was to meet her, how proud they were of the school's new name and to thank the longtime trailblazer for her work. Dr. Dolores Silas is indeed a trailblazer. She holds many firsts—she was the first Black woman to be elected to the Tacoma City Council. She was also one of the first Black teachers hired by the Tacoma Public School Board, the first Black principal in the Tacoma School District and the first Black woman in Tacoma to have a school named after her.

Josh Garcia, the superintendent of Tacoma Public Schools, said, "Today is truly bigger than all of us at the school renaming ceremony. Ram Nation [the Ram is the school's mascot] is adding an American hero to its legacy." Tacoma's mayor Victoria Woodards said, "There are little girls all across this community who will see this new name…who will be inspired by what they can be and what they can do in this community."

Silas was born in Elkhart, Indiana, in 1926. She was raised by her mother, grandmother and great-grandmother, women who set high standards for her, including the value of education and service. After high school, where she excelled, she attended the famed Tuskegee University in Alabama. Booker T. Washington founded the school, and its alumni include inventor George Washington Carver and novelist Ralph Ellison, author of *The Invisible Man*. Silas graduated in 1949 with a bachelor's degree in science. In 1962, she received her master's degree in education from the University of Arizona, and she received her doctorate in education in 1977 from the United States International University in San Diego. "I've been educated-minded all my life, and I enjoy working with youth," Silas said in an interview conducted by Jessie Koon for the Tacoma Historical Society when she was honored with the society's Star of Destiny Award.

Dr. Silas was the first Black administrator in Tacoma Public Schools. *Photograph courtesy of Dr. Silas's godson, Scott Breckinridge's, family.*

Silas began her teaching career in Gary, Indiana. She decided to move west in the 1950s and quickly landed a job with Tacoma Public Schools, first with Lister Elementary, where she was only the third Black teacher hired by the district. She enjoyed the rewards and challenges of teaching and helping students find their voice in the world.

In her speech at the school's renaming, Silas said, "As a person who was born on the wrong side of the railroad tracks, to have a school named after you—what does that tell you—that anything is possible."

Silas's dedication to teaching, her students and her beloved Hilltop neighborhood made her a beloved member of the community. Cynthia Tucker, president of the Washington Association of Colored Women's Clubs, described Silas: "Dr. Silas was a true Black woman. Her race and her culture and her community meant a lot to her. Most of the things she did involved those things."

Dr. Silas spoke at the school name-changing ceremony. The school was renamed from Woodrow Wilson High School to Dr. Dolores Silas High School in 2021. *Photograph courtesy of Dr. Silas's godson, Scott Breckinridge's, family.*

Silas was appointed the first Black principal in 1970. She worked at Delong Elementary School. "Being the first woman of color in that position was a challenge," said Silas in her Tacoma Historical Society interview. "The students, for the most part, were fine; they love you regardless. There was an education part toward teachers who were new to the world of African Americans. I'm working with teachers to help them provide for students and parents who don't know what I am. It was difficult," she said.

Silas was a leader and knew she had to make the situation work because so much was riding on her success. "The students were comfortable with me. I remember the first day of school, standing in the school's doorway, saying hello to the students, and this kindergartner came up to me and put her arms around me and said, 'Hi, how are you?' I said, 'I'm fine, thank you,' and she said, 'I don't mind that you are Black.' So, I know she had listened at home that she was going to have a Black principal. She did care," said Silas. She said she still had to make headway with the teachers and parents, however. "I think 90 percent of people accepted me there," Silas said.

Until her retirement in 1982, Silas took on leadership roles in organizations like the National Teachers Corps. The United States Congress's Higher Education Act established the organization in 1965. It was focused on improving teaching in low-income areas.

Cynthia Tucker said Silas fought hard for the schools in the Hilltop neighborhood. "The Hilltop schools didn't get a lot of money or resources, but Dr. Silas continually pushed for more money and resources for our children," she said.

Dr. Silas was the first Black woman to serve on the Tacoma City Council. *Photograph courtesy of Dr. Silas's godson, Scott Breckinridge's, family.*

After twenty-six years as a teacher, Silas changed course. After spending years looking for solutions to problems, in 1991, she was appointed to the Tacoma City Council. She ran and served two additional terms and also served as deputy mayor. "When you do something that you know is right or wrong, you can be in a comfort zone. Being the first Black woman on the city council was my uncomfortable zone," said Silas in her historical society interview. "I remember being the president of the Tacoma NAACP, standing at the microphone asking for help—and then I realized I should be on the other side of the microphone, giving help. Life is always a challenge," she said.

Silas was wellversed in the community's concerns, serving as president of the NAACP, and was actively involved in the Tacoma Human Rights Commission, the Black Collective and the Hilltop Multi-Service Center.

"I was very fortunate being on the city council. The Hilltop area had been a challenge, and I thought the area had been ignored for years. I wanted to uplift Hilltop and have others see it the way I see it," said Silas.

Cynthia Tucker said Silas took the lead in tackling challenging problems. "Whenever the council took on subjects like affordable housing, she had a way of leading the way," said Tucker. "During her years on the council, she championed for public safety, affordable housing, resources for education and neighborhood development."

Tucker said Silas was devoted to the Hilltop neighborhood, a place she had called home. Tucker explained that Silas wanted the Hilltop area to be a place where people of all incomes and races could live and be proud of the neighborhood.

Silas was not content to govern from her office, and she often took to the streets. "I was on the city council when gangs were very relevant. I did invite various gang leaders to my house to talk," said Silas. "People often said, 'You are inviting them to your house?' And I said yes, somebody has to talk to them. There was an atmosphere that there was something they needed to say, and I wanted to hear it. We would sit down at my kitchen table, and the leaders would talk to me."

Silas was a woman who embraced the world. As an avid traveler, she traveled the world, visiting other countries and embracing different cultures. Ever the devoted public servant, Silas turned her trips into fact-finding missions. She started learning about other countries' economic and governing systems, hoping to incorporate those ideas to help improve the Hilltop neighborhood.

Silas was devoted to public service. She was a member of the Tacoma chapter of the Urban League's board of directors, the YWCA's board of directors and the Delta Kappa Gamma Society, a professional society for women educators.

Silas, over the years, proved to be a savvy businesswoman. She had retail shops at the Seattle Convention Center; she was also a partner on the contract for the Washington State History Museum Café in downtown Tacoma and had concessions at the SeaTac Airport.

Silas also loved sports, especially Seahawks football. "Anyone who visited her home on weekends knew that she had all five TVs turned on to the current college or professional game," said Tucker.

"It is not what I say to you that is important—it is what you say to yourself," said Dr. Silas. *Photograph courtesy of Dr. Silas's godson, Scott Breckinridge's, family.*

Silas was known for her generosity. She willed her home to the Tacoma chapter of the Washington Association of Colored Women's Clubs. "That was so typical of Dr. Silas," said Tucker. "She knew we are trying to build a new clubhouse, and she wanted us to use the money from the sale to help." Silas was a proud member of the club. "She is a lifetime member, and of course, we will have a Dr. Dolores Silas Room in the new clubhouse," said Tucker. "She gave me several of her papers, including her doctorate dissertation, for display."

Silas was also known for her style, especially her stylish hats. Silas explained in a television interview that she had a hat for every outfit. "She wore a hat every day of her life. I visited her home, and in all three bedrooms, there were hats on the wall," said Tucker. "The club will inherit part of her hat collection. I'll have to figure out a way to encase the hats to preserve them."

On reflection of the school name change, Silas said she cried. "I am so proud and so blessed," she said. Silas said in her speech at the ceremony, "I didn't do anything for the glory. I did it because it was the right thing to do."

Dr. Dolores Silas passed away on July 24, 2021. In addition to the Tacoma Historical Society's Star of Destiny Award in 2019, she received the City of Tacoma's Lifetime Service City of Destiny Award in 2019.

16

VICTORIA FREEMAN

Longview's Civil Rights Pioneer

Victoria Freeman was a community organizer and activist in Longview.
She led the charge to desegregate Longview's public schools.

When Victoria Freeman; her husband, James; and their two sons, Oliver and Calvin, moved to Longview in 1923, Victoria was thrilled. The Freemans were one of the first Black families to move to the newly established city. Like many Black Americans, the West offered a new start and the prospect of new opportunities. Freeman, a staunch proponent of education, was excited to enroll her children in public school. "When my mother went to enroll my brothers, a teacher told her they couldn't be enrolled because they were Black," said Freeman's daughter Ruby West in an interview with Cynthia Tucker, a historian with the Washington Association of Colored Women's Clubs.

The only alternative for Black students was a tar paper shack with no chairs or desks. Freeman took one look at the school and decided it was unacceptable and sent her boys to California to live with her sister for the school year.

In 1924, Freeman decided that she wanted her boys with their family.

Freeman was not formally educated but was self-educated. She knew Washington State did not condone segregation. She arranged a meeting with J.H. Secrest, the attorney for Long-Bell Lumber, where her husband worked, and asked for advice. "My mother went to the superintendent of the school and told him that her sons were not allowed to enroll in the public school,

Freeman was an early civil rights activist and community organizer in Longview.
Photograph courtesy of Ruby West.

and it was against the law," said West. "The superintendent told my mother to take the children to Kessler and tell the teacher to put the children at a desk," said West. The school had no choice and enrolled the boys. With her determination, Freeman broke the color barrier and struck down segregation in the city of Longview. According to a newspaper report, the class teacher protested and went to the principal, insisting there was no room. The principal insisted she find room. "The teacher came back like Little Bo Peep who lost her sheep," Freeman told the reporter.

"My mother took on the issue of segregation on her own," said West. "Because of her, all Black children were allowed to attend the Longview public schools. She was the reason for the changes."

Victoria Freeman was born in Jeanerette, Louisiana, in 1894. Her grandmother, who was formerly enslaved, raised her. Her husband, James, was born in Georgia. In addition to their two sons, the Freemans added their daughters, Audrey, Inez and Ruby, to their family. Freeman didn't attend high school, but she insisted that her children receive an education. "My mother had a third-grade education. However, her uncle had paid for her to go to a private school," said West. "So, her education was equal to an eighth-grade level."

Freeman worked as a housekeeper making fifty cents an hour. "She worked part time because she wanted to be home with us," said West. "All forms of education were important to my mother. She cleaned houses so that we could take music lessons. My oldest sister, Audrey, sang, Inez played the violin and I played the piano."

Freeman was also a civil rights activist. West explained her mother worked alone most of the time. "People would seek out my mother and talk to her about various forms of discrimination in shops and restaurants," said West. Freeman became the liaison between the business owners and the community. "She was the interceder," said West.

West doesn't know how her mother encouraged the business owners to change their minds, because the children were not allowed to accompany her. Needless to say, Freeman was effective and persuasive in her talks. Once she talked with the business owners, the next day, when Black people returned to the restaurant, they could sit and eat without incident. "She would always come out of the business smiling," said West.

Although Freeman was the liaison between the Black community, businesses and schools, she wasn't formally a part of civil rights organizations, such as the NAACP. One reason for this is that the Ku Klux Klan was very active and prominent in Longview during that time. "If Blacks were involved or engaged in such organizations, it had to be kept very low-key. Only about sixty-eight Blacks were living in Longview at the time," West told Tucker.

Freeman was also a community activist and organizer and a member of the Woman's Study Club, a sister club of the Washington Association of Colored Women's Clubs. The club was established in 1950 and was devoted to community service and lifelong learning. Freeman was a member of the House of Prayer, Bible study groups, the Woman's Temperance Union and an active church worker.

Freeman took pride in her community, such as it was. She and the Women's Study Club decided that the neighborhood, where most of the Black population lived, needed to be cleaned up. "The roads were all dirt roads, there were no sidewalks, the septic system was not for Black families or the Black community to use," West said in a *Longview Daily News* article. "The alleys were atrocious with cast-offs," West said. The clubwomen decided to take matters into their own hands and organize a clean-up to make the area a safe and healthy place for the women and children. The women petitioned the city and the homeowners to help with the clean-up.

The Women's Study Club members met with city officials to determine how much the improvements would cost. "The cost was about $1,856. That was a lot of money," said West. "The women decided to cook and sell barbeque dinners." Unfortunately, the women fell short of their monetary goal. "What they raised was not enough for the massive improvements they wanted, which included having the streets paved, sidewalks put in and alleyways cleaned of garbage and debris," said West.

During that time, Sears and Roebuck Company had a community service contest. The women applied and were ecstatic that they had won first prize. The clubwomen and the mayor of Longview received an all-expense-paid trip to Washington, D.C., to accept the prize money. "The award money was about $6,000 and enabled the clubwomen to complete their improvements," said West. The women had enough money to buy an additional block of land from the city between Douglas and Delaware Streets. "With the help of the city park director, they cleaned up the block and made a nice park," said

Victoria Freeman Park was renamed to honor Freeman's work in Longview. *Photograph courtesy of Longview Metro Parks.*

West. "My mom was so proud because the kids in the neighborhood had a clean and safe place to play."

The women decided to name the area Clearview Park "because of the clear view of the land from the park to downtown; no trees were interfering with the view," said West.

In 1994, the City of Longview renamed the park Victoria Freeman Park. The 6.5-acre park's amenities include basketball courts, a sports field, shelters and a playground. The park honors and is a lasting legacy to the trailblazing woman who fought to desegregate schools and the city of Longview. "The park is a lasting, tangible legacy to my mother," said West.

Freeman was the mother of five children. She also had twenty-three grandchildren and thirty-six great-grandchildren at the time of this writing. In 1970, Freeman was named Washington's Mother of the Year.

Victoria Freeman passed away in 1994 at one hundred years old. Cynthia Tucker summed up the enormity of Victoria Freeman's contribution to the city of Longview: "She was a community activist, spokesperson, city negotiator, peacemaker, fundraiser and mover and shaker. Victoria Freeman and her tenacity changed the early history of the city of Longview."

17

MANIMA WILSON

The First Black Woman to Graduate from Everett High School and the University of Washington

Manima Wilson was the first Black woman to graduate from Everett High School in 1907. She graduated with honors and is believed to be the first Black woman to graduate from the University of Washington.

Manima Wilson was encouraged by her parents to get an education. They believed that education was the road to success for Black Americans seeking a better life. Wilson was born in 1886 in Everett, Washington, the only child to parents Arminta Spears Wilson and Samuel Wilson, a Baptist minister. Wilson was the first Black woman to graduate from Everett High School in 1907. She was reportedly an excellent student who was well liked by her teachers.

Wilson was also believed to be the first Black woman to graduate from the University of Washington, where she received her bachelor's degree.

Her mother, Arminta, was a clubwoman who was devoted to club and charity work. She was a chapter member of the Washington Association of Colored Women's Clubs in Spokane and Everett.

Information about Wilson's adult years is vague, but she took up her mother's mantle and became involved in community and charity work. She worked with Seattle's Central Area Sojourner Truth Home. The Sojourner Truth Home was founded in 1919 and located at 1422 Twenty-Third Avenue. Due to the growing number of Black people moving to Washington, there was an increasing need for social services. The organization was vital to the Black community, intending to help

Top: Everett High School in the early days. *Photograph courtesy of Jack O'Donnell.*

Bottom: Manima Wilson on her graduation day in 1907. *Photograph courtesy of the Black Heritage Society of Washington State Inc., 2001.11.2.11.*

with critical needs, such as temporary housing, food and healthcare. The organization was active for more than twenty years.

The house was named after Sojourner Truth, the iconic abolitionist and civil and women's rights advocate. She was born into slavery in 1797 as Isabella Baumfree in New York. She was sold several times during her childhood. In 1779, New York decided to legislate the end of slavery. Truth's master had promised to free her on July 4, 1826, before the law went into effect. He reneged on his promise, and Truth escaped with her youngest daughter. Truth explained, "I didn't run away. I walked away in daylight."

In 1843, she changed her name to Sojourner Truth, telling her friends, "The Lord gave me truth because I was to declare truth to people." Truth became one the most prominent voices of the abolitionist and civil and women's rights movements. She went to court in 1843 seeking custody of her son, who was still in slavery, and won. She became the first Black woman to win a case of this kind.

Truth met with President Abraham Lincoln on October 29, 1864. That was quite an achievement for a formerly enslaved person. In her autobiography, Truth wrote, "I said I appreciate you, for you are the best president who has ever taken the seat....I then said I had never heard of him before he was talked of for president. He smilingly replied, 'I had heard of you many times before that.'"

At a women's rights convention in Akron, Ohio, in 1851, Sojourner Truth delivered her famous "Ain't I a Woman?" speech. In the speech, she spoke of women's rights, human rights and dignity. It became an anthem for many Black women.

18

ROSA FRANKLIN

The First Black Woman Elected to the Washington State Senate

Rosa Franklin spent her life in service. After 42 years as a nurse, Franklin entered politics and became the first African American woman elected as a state senator, serving from 1993 to 2011. She was also a delegate to the Democratic National Conventions in 1976 and 1988.

Rosa Franklin made history by becoming the first Black woman to serve and be elected into the Washington State Senate. Ironically, that almost didn't happen. After the trailblazer retired from nursing, she devoted herself to volunteering for various political organizations to improve her Tacoma community. She explains in the book *Rosa Franklin: A Life in Healthcare, Public Service, and Social Justice*, by Tamiko Nimura, released by the Washington State legislature's oral history program, she was reluctant to run for office. "One day, I got this call from Rosie Hargrove, Twenty-Ninth District chair, who informed me that P.J. Gallagher would not be seeking reelection and asked me to run—my answer was no," said Franklin. "Rosie kept after me until I said yes." And as the saying goes, the rest was history. Franklin was elected to the House of Representatives in 1990, representing the Twenty-Ninth District. She won re-election in 1992. However, when the state senator from the Twenty-Ninth District died unexpectedly, Franklin was appointed to complete the term, making her the first Black woman to serve as a state senator. The following year, Franklin ran for the position and made history again by becoming the first Black woman elected as a state senator in Washington. She ran unopposed for three successive elections.

Rosa Franklin was the first Black woman to become a state senator. *Photograph courtesy of Washington State Archives.*

In her oral history story, Franklin's assistant, Annette Swillie, described Franklin as a fierce campaigner. "She worked day and night on her campaign. She took time to talk with her supporters, wanting to know what they had to say."

Franklin's parents were Henrietta Bryant, a homemaker, and James Guidrion, who worked for the Works Progress Administration. In her oral history, Franklin described her upbringing as loving but poor. When she was seven, she lived with her aunt and uncle in Georgetown, South Carolina, but returned to her parents' home in the summer.

Franklin came from a family that valued education. She graduated from Howard High School in Georgetown in 1944. She attended the University of South Carolina before entering the cadet nursing program at Good Samaritan Waverly Hospital in Columbia, South Carolina, graduating in 1948.

Franklin met her husband, James, at a USO dance while stationed at Fort Jackson, North Carolina, where she attended nursing school. They were married in 1950. After their wedding, he was assigned to Fort Dix in New Jersey. Franklin worked at a state hospital in New Jersey. When her husband was transferred to Germany, she moved to New York and worked at the Brooklyn Jewish Hospital and Medical Center. Healthcare became her passion. She worked with newborns, people with mental illnesses, women from all walks of life and military personnel. In the University of Washington's Tacoma History Project oral history interview, she said that there was a shortage of nurses during World War II. Even though she was not in the military, there was a recruitment of nurses and nursing students to help in the war effort.

Franklin moved to Germany to join her husband. She always dreamed of being a world traveler, as she told writer Elizabeth Walter of the University of Washington's Tacoma Community History Project. Unlike in the segregated South, in Germany, Franklin was welcomed at restaurants, hotels, museums and other venues. She felt what equality was like. The Franklins moved several places before relocating back in Tacoma, where they settled.

After returning to Tacoma to live and while working and raising children, Franklin returned to school. She received bachelor's degrees in biology and English from the University of Puget Sound, graduated in 1968 and earned her master's degree in social sciences and human relations from Pacific Lutheran University. She also earned a certificate from the University of Washington Gynecorp Training Program and was awarded an honorary doctorate from the University of Puget Sound.

While working as a nurse at a Hilltop Children's clinic, she became an outreach coordinator. "My job was to go from door to door within a defined area in order to get children in the clinic," she said in the oral history project. "I was brought up to be involved. Me going into nursing was a natural fit, me being from a caring about the welfare of the community type of family." After a forty-two-year career, Franklin retired from nursing.

Franklin explained in her oral history, "I come from a family of involvement. They were people who tried to help, not content just to sit back and complain."

Franklin began volunteering for the Democratic Party and the League of Women Voters. The League of Women Voters is a nonpartisan political women's group that works on public issues. "I loved working with that group," she said in the UW interview. She was also involved with the Tacoma Urban League, NAACP, Safe Streets and the Cancer Screening Programs.

Franklin sought public office for the first time in 1972, when she ran for a seat for the Tacoma City Council and lost. She wasn't deterred by the loss and continued her involvement with politics. She was devoted to the Democratic Party. Franklin was a delegate for the Democratic National Conventions in 1976, 1988 and 2008. Franklin decided she wanted to do more to serve her community and decided to run for office again in 1990. She ran for a seat in the House of Representatives. Her house served as her campaign headquarters. "It was an uphill battle," she said in her oral history. "The goal was to outreach and bring in volunteers who had never been involved with politics and had a diverse group of supporters. I knew the district."

The political establishment didn't give her much of a chance. Her opponent didn't put up much of a campaign, confident that he would win handily. "He didn't do much campaigning," Franklin said in her oral history. Her doubters underestimated the indefatigable political novice. She defeated her opponent in a landslide—8,050 votes to 3,535.

While in the Senate, Franklin poured herself into her duties, like most endeavors in her life. Her committee assignments included the Committees of Financial Institutions, Housing, Insurance, Health and Long-Term Care and Rules. Her focus centered on equal housing, social justice and equal access to healthcare.

Franklin established the Governor's Intragency Council on Health Disparities. Its mission statement reads: "We are committed to promoting equality for all historically marginalized communities....However, we recognize that racism is ingrained in our history and deeply embedded in our institutions."

"I've always tried to get involved with healthcare," Franklin said in the UW Tacoma project. "I've always tried to get people involved with their healthcare, [especially] people who have traditionally been left out, such as people of color and poor people....As for healthcare, I keep saying, when you have healthcare, you also increase your profits. You will not have people out because they are sick, [therefore] minimizing your healthcare costs."

In Franklin's first year in the Senate, she sponsored a bill that became the Washington Housing Policy Act. "When I ran for city council in 1972, that was my platform," she said in her oral history. "You cannot have a viable city unless you have healthy people. Your environment, housing, everything is dependent on this. Some people aren't forward-thinking. You have to think about the future. If you don't do that, you have to go back and try to fix it, and by that time, you've lost ground."

Franklin had many leadership roles while in the Washington State Senate. She served as majority whip and Democratic whip, and in her second term, she was elected president pro-tempore, commonly called pro-tem. The president pro-tem is the second-highest-ranking leader in the house. The president pro-tem presides over the Senate chamber in the absence of the president. The position also ensures members follow all rules and procedures. Being elected pro-tem, Franklin made history again by being the first Black person and the first Black woman to hold the position in Washington. Franklin was excited to be in the role. "When you have the gavel, you are in control of the Senate," she said. "They cannot do anything unless you let it happen. You have to keep your view cast on everyone so that you serve the whole process."

Franklin said her colleagues in the Senate always treated her with respect and dignity. According to her oral history, they also thought she was an effective and efficient legislator. "Being effective means that I can't do it by myself. I have to work with someone else, collaborating," she said. "When you are in a leadership role, you are setting an example. If you are going to set an example for those who want to follow, what kind of example do you want to set?"

In her oral history, Annette Swillie said Franklin's work ethic was unprecedented and that she was totally devoted to governing. She usually came to work at 7:30 a.m. and stayed until 10:00 p.m.

When reflecting on being the first Black woman in the Senate, Franklin said, "Well, you know that they're looking at you thinking, 'What's going to come out of your mouth?' I put on my best." Reflecting on her time in the Senate, she said, "My focus was not just being there but being there to make a difference."

In 2010, after twenty years of serving in the legislature, Franklin decided to retire. In part of her resignation letter to her colleagues and staff, she wrote, "It is difficult to say I am retiring from the Senate. Therefore, I'll just say I am not seeking re-election. I will miss the fast pace of legisltive sessions and debates on public policy. I plan to continue working to make our communities, state and nation live up to the principles on which they were founded, and the constitution represents all of us and not a select few. Remember always to be brave and take risks. That is the only way change is made."

Retiring from the Senate didn't mean Franklin stopped being involved. "When I retired, I said I was going back to my community, and that's essentially what I'm doing," she said in her oral history.

Franklin left a lasting legacy. She was a mentor to other legislators and people in the community from all walks of life.

Franklin has been married to her husband, James, since 1950. They have three children, and they also have grandchildren.

Franklin is not done making history. When she learned that the Franklin Park in Tacoma, named after founding father Benjamin Franklin, would be renamed Senator Rosa Franklin Park, her first reaction was, "Are you sure?" She asked King 5 news, laughing. "I wasn't expecting this. I am humbled and honored." Onlookers greeted Franklin with hugs and applause at the name-changing ceremony.

The Metro Parks Board of Commissions in Tacoma unanimously voted to change the park's name to honor the trailblazer. The park is the first park in Tacoma named after a Black woman. "Thank you so much, and thank you for this honor," she said at the ceremony.

Aaron Pointer, the Metro Parks Board's commissioner, said at the name-changing ceremony, "Senator Franklin is without question an outstanding individual, who forged a path for herself through adversity and built connections to advance the cause of social justice, healthcare and racial equality in Tacoma and throughout Washington State."

Rosa Franklin at the renaming ceremony of the Senator Rosa Franklin Park in Tacoma, Washington. *Photograph courtesy of Tacoma Metro Parks Department.*

Franklin received many awards during her public life, including a Lifetime Achievement Award from the Washington State Democratic Party in 2000. The Washington State Nurses Association inducted her into its hall of fame in 2002. In 2006, she received an honorary doctorate in public service, and in 2019, she received the MLK Dream Award from the University of Washington, Tacoma.

"I have great hope for the future," Franklin said at the ceremony. "I'm not finished yet. At ninety-four, I'm still going."

19

FABIENNE "FAE" BROOKS

Trailblazing Law Enforcement Officer

Fae Brooks has a long string of firsts with the King County Sheriff's Department, including being the first Black officer to attend the FBI Academy, the first Black woman detective and the first Black woman hired as a commissioned deputy.

Retired King County deputy Fae Brooks recalled one of her cases in her long law enforcement career. "It was one of my early cases. A rape suspect had left his wallet in the back seat of the woman's car," said Brooks. "I called him pretending I had just found the wallet. He was eager for me to come down to his place of employment to return his wallet. He was surprised that we placed him under arrest. He was even more surprised when I asked him if he knew where he lost his wallet," she said. That was a relatively straightforward case for the trailblazing law enforcement officer. During her twenty-six-year-long career, Brooks racked up a number of firsts that read like a who's who among law enforcement officers.

Brooks was the first Black woman to attend Washington State Law Enforcement Command College. She was the first Black woman to attend the FBI National Academy (located in Quantico, Virginia) from the state of Washington. Brooks is also the first Black woman detective and the first Black woman hired as a commissioned deputy withing the King County Sheriff's Office. Brooks retired as chief of the Criminal Division for King County's Sheriff's Office. "I didn't realize that I was the first Black woman commissioned deputy officer when I was hired," said Brooks. "I didn't know that I was making history."

Brooks was the only Black person and only woman in her academy graduation class on October 13, 1978. *Photograph courtesy of Fae Brooks.*

"I was the only Black and the only woman in my academy class," said Brooks. In the 1970s, the sheriff's office hired women as jail matrons or juvenile detectives—not officers. Brooks finished second in her class at the police academy. She would have been first in her class but had never fired a weapon before and did not score well in that area. Brooks said most of her classmates at the academy were very supportive of her, often running with her during training and giving her tips on climbing the wall.

Brooks became a member of the sex crime unit in 1980. "At the time, there were three detectives in the sex crime unit—all males," said Brooks. "The sheriff's office decided to expand the office after pressure from the Rape Relief Organization. The unit of three detectives was doubled by adding three—two women and one man. I am a survivor of childhood sexual abuse, so I think I was effective with the victims. I could empathize with them," Brooks said. Ironically, her status even helped with getting confessions.

Perhaps Brooks's most memorable time with the sheriff's office was when she became one of the original detectives on the Green River Killer case. For more than twenty years, a serial killer known as the Green River Killer terrorized the citizens of King County by systematically raping and murdering young women, many of them prostitutes and runaways, and scattering their bodies throughout King County. The killer, eventually identified as Gary Ridgeway, an unassuming truck painter, was initially convicted of forty-eight murders. "I joined the task force in 1982," said Brooks. "The case was all-consuming. To this day, there are places I drive through in King County, and it takes me back to that time." Brooks distinctly remembers when one of the victims was identified; Brooks had had a prior connection to the woman from the sex crime unit. "The victim was a victim of another crime, and she decided not to press charges but then became a victim of the Green River Killer. It hit me hard. I'm actually thankful I wasn't at the scene when they recovered her body. The victims live on with you—they become close to you in a certain way."

Brooks was a member of the task force until 1989. What she remembers about the manhunt for the Green River Killer was the officers' passion for solving the case. "I can close my eyes now and see the pictures of the victims on the wall. We kept saying we are going to get this guy. I remember the buzz and activities surrounding the case," said Brooks.

Brooks said when detectives finally arrested Gary Ridgeway, he confessed to killing forty-eight or forty-nine women. "There were a few

Brooks's recruitment photograph with a dog in 1979. *Photograph courtesy of Fae Brooks.*

other victims that we couldn't find," said Brooks. His confession of killing forty-eight women marked him as the second-most-productive serial killer in American history.

Working on sex crime cases and the Green River Killer case, Brooks said she had to be mindful of the rule of compartmentalizing. "You live like in the TV shows; the best thing to do is leave work at work and don't bring it home," she said. "What I had been through prepared me while I was working the sex crime cases."

Brooks left her mark on the criminal justice system in a very unusual way when she coined the phrase "person of interest." The term is such a significant contribution that it has become part of the language of law enforcement. You hear the phrase in law enforcement press conferences; you hear it on television shows and true crime shows. Brooks said she came up with the term around 1986. "I'm very proud of that," said Brooks. "Back then, we were investigating a suspect who was not quite a suspect. He was a person we were interested in. Rather than calling him a suspect, he became a 'person of interest.'" Brooks said when she's introducing herself to law enforcement groups, she tells them where the phrase originated. "It feels wonderful to have made that contribution," Brooks said.

Brooks was born in Harlem, New York, into a naval military family. Her father, John Wood, was in the navy and from Kentucky. Her mother, Vyola Prince Wood, was a bank teller who was born in Washington, D.C. They met in New York City. She is the oldest of three children. As a child in a military family, she had the opportunity to travel extensively. She attended many schools, including schools in Kansas, New York, Connecticut and Japan, and she spent the last part of her senior year in Alaska. "The benefit of that is I got to meet so many people," said Brooks. When she was growing up, she often visited her great-grandmother, who lived in Washington, D.C. Brooks remembers always wanting to be in law enforcement. She remembers her great-uncle (her great-grandmother's brother) was a police officer in Washington, D.C. "When I was there, I remember him coming down the stairs in his uniform. He was so tall and good-looking," said Brooks. " He was also the first Black law enforcement person to attend the FBI Academy, and he retired as deputy chief of the Washington, D.C Metropolitan Police Department. As a result, I always had an excellent impression of policing."

Brooks moved to Bellingham in 1969 to attend Western Washington University. She had an array of jobs before moving into law enforcement. In high school, during the summers and on weekends, she worked as a movie guard for the children's matinee at the movie theater on the naval base. She also worked as a children's pool lifeguard on the base during the summers.

Brooks worked at *Ebony Magazine* (Johnson's Publishing Company) in New York in customer service.

Brooks also worked as an investigator for the Public Defenders' Association as a secretary, investigator, executive secretary to the defender and office manager for the Juvenile Division.

Before Brooks became a deputy sheriff, she worked as the office manager for the Juvenile Division, where she met her husband, a firefighter with the Seattle Fire Department. "Two firefighters came into the office to conduct an annual inspection, and later on that afternoon, I got a call from one of them with follow-up questions. I found out later that he knew the answers; he just wanted to meet me," said Brooks. They have known each other for forty-four years and have been married for forty-two (at the time of this writing). Her husband retired as a captain for the fire department after thirty-two years of service. They have four children, ten grandchildren and three great-grandchildren.

Brooks said one of her first mentors was her grandmother. "She told me that I could do anything I put my mind to, and I used that mantra during my police career," she said in the *FBI NAA Newsletter* "Exceptional Member" article. "I've had several mentors during my life; men, women, Black, white, who all encouraged me during various times in my career."

Her grandmother's words were dear to her when she started her law enforcement career. "My college roommate knew I always wanted to be in law enforcement. Coincidentally, she worked for the sheriff's office in King County and called to let me know the agency was recruiting for commissioned officers. She told me, 'You know you always wanted to work in law enforcement.'" Brooks applied in 1977 and passed the written and physical tests. Brooks said she had a mentor who gave her support for the physical fitness part of the examination. "At first, I wasn't on the certification list when it was published. During that time, women and men were graded differently for the physical fitness part of the examination. When the error was discovered, the test score was corrected, and it was determined that I had, in fact, passed."

Brooks at a recruiting event in 1988. *Photograph courtesy of Fae Brooks.*

As her career progressed, the sheriff's department saw her potential and nominated Brooks to attend the FBI Academy in 1995. The coursework centered on leadership, current trends, physical training, legal decisions and community policing, one of Brooks's passions. "The coursework was interesting, and networking with other law enforcement professionals from around the world was so beneficial," said Brooks.

In 1997, Brooks was an Atlantic Fellow in Public Policy assigned in London. "I was studying equality policies in the United States (where it is required) and the United Kingdom (where it was not) and documented the differences," she said. There, she conducted training on policing for safer communities, policing through partnerships and diversity.

Fae Brooks has a long string of firsts in the King County Sheriff's Department, including being the first Black officer to attend the FBI Academy. *Photograph courtesy of Fae Brooks.*

Brooks's other first Black woman achievements in the King County Sheriff's Office included being the first Black woman to become detective, media relations officer, sergeant, captain, major and chief. She was also the first Black woman and the first Black person appointed to the rank of division chief.

Brooks said a senior patrol deputy and fellow gave her the best advice: "A sense of humor was crucial in this job," she said in the FBI newsletter.

Brooks has also helped develop policies and directives on unbiased policing and domestic violence involving law enforcement officers during her career.

Brooks retired from the King County Sheriff's Department in 2004. Brooks is now president and CEO of Brooks' Strategic Assessment and Communication Inc. Her company specializes in training and building community partnerships.

She has continued to work in law enforcement by embarking on a new career focus. She's been a consultant for many national and international organizations since 2004. She developed training in diversity and communication skills for law enforcement, both nationally and internationally. "Community and police can and should be in partnership together by trust-building and exploring implicit biases," said Brooks.

Brooks has also designed a curriculum specifically for Washington State law enforcement. She's served as the community project coordinator for

NCBI/COPS and Community Program in King County. She was also a cochair of the King County Executive's Inquest Process Review Committee. In addition, Brooks also served as policy adviser for the mayor of Seattle on community/police engagement.

Brooks is a member of the board of several organizations, including the Domestic Abuse Women's Network, King County Sexual Assault Resource Center, Seattle Neighborhood Group and the Park Lake/White Center Boys and Girls Club.

Brooks is the past president (and first Black woman to serve in that role) of the Black Law Enforcement Association of Washington, a lifetime member of the NAACP, a lifetime member of the National Organization of Black Law Enforcement Executives and a member (and past chapter president and first Black woman to serve in that role) of the Washington State Chapter of the FBI National Academy Associates. She is a member of the African Methodist Episcopal (AME) church.

Brooks was asked in the FBI newsletter if there was one thing she would have changed about her job. She answered, "I would have incorporated authentic communication training for law enforcement on a national level. I believe the benefit of improved relationships with members of law enforcement and community residents has a lasting impact on both groups."

"I loved my career, and I loved my job. If I had to do it all over again—I would," said Brooks. "I think I did an excellent job in separating home and my job. My kids would say when I was home, I was Mom."

20

THE WOMEN WHO PROPELLED THE SEATTLE CHAPTER OF THE CONGRESS OF RACIAL EQUALITY (CORE)

During the 1960s, the Seattle chapter of CORE (Congress of Racial Equality) was one of the city's most prolific civil rights organizations. The multiracial organization, through selective campaigns, led protests against employers who discriminated against minorities. The organization fought for open housing and education parity.

The civil rights movement was alive and well in Seattle during the early 1960s and well before. Organizations like the NAACP, the Central Area Civil Rights Committee and the Congress of Racial Equality (CORE) campaigned and protested for equal employment, housing and education rights. Women were often on the front lines of organizations, as was the case with CORE.

CORE was founded in 1942 at the University of Chicago and became one of the nation's leading civil rights organizations.

The Seattle chapter of CORE launched in the 1950s but didn't get off the ground. In 1961, four women, Bettylou Valentine, Joan Singler, Jean "Maid" Adams and Jean Durning, propelled the organization as leaders and committee chairs. They strategized campaigns and protests using a three-prong approach—research, negotiation and protest—that was vital to bringing about racial diversity.

Bettylou Valentine, Joan Singler and Maid Adams recounted their stories in the oral history of the Seattle Civil Rights and Labor History Project.

In its early years, Seattle was a segregated town with little to no integration in housing, employment, schools or even public transportation through the late 1960s. Bettylou Valentine had moved to Seattle from Pittsburg in 1959 to attend graduate school. She was surprised by the lack of diversity in Seattle. "It was much more segregated than Pittsburg," she said. "I felt it was a distinct society. There were other people, but they were not connected," she said in the oral history of the Seattle Civil Rights and Labor History Project. Seattle neighborhoods were segregated; Black people were barred from jobs in major department stores, especially those downtown, grocery stores and schools.

Bettylou Valentine was one of the leaders of CORE in Seattle. *Photograph courtesy of the Museum of History and Industry.*

Before moving to Seattle, Valentine was a longtime civil rights activist who explained that her parents were a mixed-race couple married in the 1930s. "That was not a particularly nice place to be, so my father's response to that was to be as uncolored as possible. When I got involved with civil rights issues, my father was not happy about it," she said. "He used to send me newspaper clippings and said, 'Your people are acting up again.'"

Despite her father's concerns, Valentine got involved with the civil rights movement and was the youth representative on the National Board of Directors of the NAACP. "When I came out here in 1959, I tried to start a chapter of the NAACP on campus, but the authorities said no and that it was not relevant to academics," she said.

The civil rights landscape changed in 1961, when the Seattle chapter of CORE was formed. Although at the time, the national chapter didn't sanction the Seattle chapter. CORE became a strong civil rights organization with its philosophy of investigating, negotiating and acting. It effectively brought to light the discriminatory practices against Black people and people of color. CORE is credited with changing the landscape of how realtors, employers and schools operate in Seattle. Valentine, Durning, Singler and Adams are credited with propelling the organization into producing effective and needed change. Valentine was Black, and the others were white women who wrote a book titled *Seattle in Black and White: The Congress of Racial Equality and the Fight for Equal Opportunity*, in which they recounted their experiences. Singler, who was part of CORE before Valentine, said CORE has always been an integrated organization that made for a powerful coalition. Singler said multiracial community involvement played a critical role in CORE's success.

Singler said a film showing what the Freedom Riders went through in their bus rides down to the southern states also sparked interest and energized interest and membership in CORE. "The film of the Freedom Riders, which showed the burning of the buses, was sent to twenty-five cities across the country, and Seattle was one of those cities. By that time, Ray Cooper, a Freedom Rider from Seattle, was back in town and would do talks," she said. "My husband and I went to the Tri-Cities, which was a segregated town, and showed the film, and it sparked interest there. A CORE chapter was formed there."

The Seattle CORE adopted the practices of the civil rights movement, led by Dr. Martin Luther King Jr., of nonviolence, sit-ins and protests. Valentine admits that she had reservations about the nonviolence rule. "My personal feeling was that I was committed to being nonviolent when I was doing a CORE activity, but I was not committed to nonviolence forever in all circumstances," she said.

Jobs discrimination in downtown department stores and grocery stores was a major concern for CORE. Following its first edict of investigation, CORE discovered that most industries, including banking, department stores and grocery stores, were places where Black people did business, but they had no or next to no Black employees. Grocery stores had the worst record. CORE's second mandate was to negotiate.

CORE and its coalition began negotiating with Safeway on September 20, 1961. Adams said the team of negotiators was a broad alliance consisting of one member from CORE, one member from the NAACP, one member from the Black Minister Alliance and one member from the Greater Council of Churches. "The ministers were our lifeline," said Adams. "They really got the word out." But the grocery chain was adamant in its stance about not hiring Black employees. CORE led the way with a "Selective Buying Campaign," informing the public. "We distributed leaflets saying don't shop where you can't work," said Singler. The leaflets worked, and Safeway started hiring Black employees in their stores. According to Historylink.org, within sixteen months, Safeway had hired twenty-eight Black employees. The "Selective Buying Campaign" was a success, and other grocery chains were also on board.

However, grocery chains A&P and Tradewell were holdouts. The stores had initially agreed to hire Black workers in negotiations but did not follow through. CORE acted by instituting a shop-in protest. "This was one of my favorite activities," said Valentine. "We would get enough people to fill the store with CORE shoppers and use every shopping cart and fill the cart full of perishables and nonbreakable items at peak hours. Then we would go to check out and ask the cashier or whoever, 'Do you hire negroes?' The answer was usually no, or I don't know. Then the shopper would say, 'I don't think I want to buy these products at your store because you discriminate.' We had taken all the carts, so no one coming in could shop until the store restocked all those items."

Singler said CORE had a picket line. "When CORE went into a store, we made sure we knew our tenets. Research and investigation were very important, and we followed those tenets to the letter of the law," she said. "We didn't want the big community to say that's not true. We knew more about stores like Safeway better than the stores themselves."

Singler said they picketed A&P in 1963. "We had a picket line at A&P every Friday, Saturday and Sunday from September through December," she said. "We chose an A&P that was close to First AME Church, where we could go and get warm and get a cup of coffee," she said.

Maid Adams was a stay-at-home mom who grew up in Wyoming, and her family had moved around a lot. "I'm so grateful that I had a lot of contact with children my age of different backgrounds of which I thought nothing of it. But it set something in place for me that I am very grateful for," she said. "In terms of awareness, I realized that there were prejudiced people in the world, and I thought they were ignorant. I had a limited understanding of racism." Adams said she thought about the implications of racism when she and her husband bought a home. The process took so long she thought their loan would be denied. It made her think about what minorities go through. "I went to a political meeting at Jean Durning's house, and I knew I wanted to get involved. I didn't know what group to join, and Wing Luke, the first person of color on the Seattle City Council, was there, and he suggested CORE." She participated in the picketing. "It was not very natural for me holding that big sign, but I did it," said Adams.

Adams said one of the many attributes of CORE was that it had people from all walks of life, and each had something unique to offer. "If someone needed to picket and had children, she could call another mom to babysit," she said.

The protests resulted in A&P finally hiring Black workers in their stores. The Shop-Ins also worked at Tradewell.

Bettylou Valentine in 1964. *Photograph courtesy of the Seattle Archives.*

CORE started working with downtown department stores. "We started with JC Penney, and the negotiations went well, and the store began hiring Blacks," said Singler.

Negotiations with other department stores resulted in a different story in opening the doors to hiring minorities. "Nordstrom had Black elevator operators, and the Bon Marche (now Macy's) had a restaurant with Black waiters, but both stores still wouldn't hire Black store clerks," said Singler. "We went to Elmer Nordstrom, and he said, 'I can't hire Blacks in our shoe department because no one would come in and buy shoes from them, and no one in the city has Black people working in their stores," said Singler. We told him that JC Penny did, and the store hadn't suffered any lost sales.

In 1961, after seeing the play *Raisin in the Sun* at the Cirque Playhouse in Madrona, Joan Singler and her husband, Ed, knew they wanted to get involved in civil rights. According to the book *Seattle in Black and White*, the Singlers met two strangers, Ken Rose and Ray Cooper, a Freedom Rider from Seattle. They were inspired by the play's message and began to discuss the violence suffered by the Freedom Riders and the pervasive segregation in Seattle. The four decided they had to do something, resulting in the beginnings of CORE.

The goal of DEED (Drive for Equal Employment in Downtown Seattle) was to increase Black employment in all businesses in downtown Seattle. Research conducted by Valentine's husband, Dr. Charles Valentine, who worked in the Anthropology Department at the University of Washington, wrote two studies that concluded Black workers had less than 3.5 percent of the jobs in downtown Seattle. "We planned a huge boycott," said Valentine. "We planned to protest in October 1964—pre-Christmas when the stores made the most money." CORE had buses that were ready to take shoppers to University Village to do their shopping. "The buses ran every hour with a sign that read 'If you want to shop, don't shop downtown, don't eat downtown,'" said Singler. In the end, CORE had delivered its goal. According to the book *Seattle in Black and White*, for two years, CORE's effort garnered more than 250 jobs for Black workers—more than any federal, state or city agency. "I think our biggest accomplishment was employment integration," said Adams.

Plagued by racial redlining from the city's very beginnings, segregated housing had been a legacy of Seattle. According to Quintard Taylor, a historian of Black history, in 1965, eight out of ten Black residents lived in the Central District. "People were not burning crosses on people's lawns, but housing was not available," said Valentine. She recounts her own housing problem when she first moved to Seattle in 1959. "As a grad student, I was looking for housing and found that was almost impossible," said Valentine. "A friend of mine lived in Queen Anne, but that didn't work out. The Ballard neighborhood was absolutely off-limits. Even the Black student athletes didn't live on campus. They went home and lived in the Central District."

The Fair Housing Act was not passed until 1968. Before then, discrimination in housing was a standard business practice. "Open housing simply meant that housing should be available to anyone who could afford it," said Valentine.

To expose the bias in the Seattle housing industry, CORE instituted Operation Window-Shop. "We would send out teams to look at homes for sale," said Valentine. "We would send out a Black couple to see the house and ask about purchasing the home or living there, but somehow, the house was not available. Of course, when we sent out the white team to the same place, it was available. I can't remember…one time that we sent out Blacks to an apartment rental that the Black person got the rental, but 90 percent of the whites got their rentals," she said.

The real estate industry was the cause of a lot of the dissension. "The industry had devised a smear campaign called forced housing," said Singler. "They told homeowners that if you voted for open housing, you are signing away your right to do with your property as you wish. The flyers they put out read: Equal rights for all vote no on forced housing."

CORE protesting for fair housing in 1964. *Photograph courtesy of the Seattle Archives.*

Singler said a concerted effort was made to convince home buyers that integrated neighborhoods were terrible for homeowners. There were newspaper advertisements that told homeowners they had a right to their privacy, the right to choose their friends and the right to sell their property to whomever they chose. "It was a scare tactic used over and over again on issues like this," said Singler. "Then there is the 'special privilege' argument where it said you have the right to enjoy your property without interference by laws giving special privileges to any group or groups."

An open housing initiative was placed on the ballot on March 10, 1964, and was defeated by a 2-to-1 margin. "I don't think two-thirds of people in Seattle were bigots, just frightened and misled," said Adams. "If there were some reservations about having Black neighbors, then you had the real estate board saying you are giving up your rights." In 1968, housing for Black individuals and other minorities were opening up in white areas. "One of the things I remember is rejoicing when someone [Black person] got a house on the Eastside or any home where Black people had never lived before," said Singler.

Transportation was also a big issue in Seattle. "There would not be an integrated taxicab system if not for CORE," said Adams. Before CORE's intervention, there were no Black taxicab drivers, bus drivers or delivery drivers. "We got involved with the port authority because they had the airport contract," said Valentine.

One of the crucial issues was the transit system. It was a public service that didn't serve all of the public, specifically the crosstown bus, better known as the number 48 that went from the Central District to the University District. There was no direct bus route, which made it difficult for Black people, particularly students living in the Central District. They had to transfer at least once downtown.

"When we approached the transit system, they said there was no need for a bus in that area, or we don't have any money for that route," said Adams. The transit system also argued that money was needed to run buses for other routes that had more traffic. As usual, CORE did its research. "We mobilized all these people to ride buses at all different times to document ridership," said Adams. "I remember riding a bus from downtown to Queen Anne Hill at 2:00 a.m. and documenting that there was no one riding the bus. We were very systemic, doing it during the day, during the evening and into very early in the morning, documenting how many people were riding those buses. The findings were written, and we were able to get a crosstown bus."

School desegregation was also an initiative of CORE. Efforts to desegregate Seattle schools were long and arduous processes. The barrier to school integration stemmed from housing discrimination that effectively centered most Black residents in one area. After the NAACP filed a lawsuit against the school board in 1961, the board developed a voluntary racial transfer program. White and Black students could voluntarily transfer to different schools. It was an attempt to combat segregation. The volunteer program didn't work. In 1964, CORE members and other civil rights groups began making negotiations to integrate schools. CORE had proposed picketing and, finally, a two-day boycott of the Seattle public schools. Students could attend "Freedom Schools" held in churches, such as Mt. Zion Baptist Church, the YMCA and other locations. The boycott was a rousing success, with more than four thousand students boycotting the public schools and opting for the "Freedom Schools." Of the students boycotting, it was estimated that at least 30 percent of the students boycotting were white. The civil rights organizations deemed the boycott a success.

In contrast, the school board and others didn't agree. According to the book *Seattle in Black and White*, media attention motivated the school board to combat segregation by instating diversity training for teachers, hiring more Black teachers and administrators and including Black history in the school's curriculum.

Historylink.org summed up the contribution of these women by stating: "The work of these four women and the other members of the organization did much to change practices and attitudes regarding race in Seattle. In less than a decade, they made Seattle a different and a better place for both white and Black people."

21

BLACK WOMEN MUSICIANS WERE THE BACKBONE IN ESTABLISHING THE BLACK MUSICIANS' UNION

The (AFM) Local 493 union was established in 1918 for Black musicians because they were shut out from joining the powerful white union (the 458). Women such as Gertrude Harvey Wright and Edythe Turnham worked hard to help establish the union.

When people think of the Seattle music scene today, they likely think of grunge music, with stars like the late Kurt Cobain leading the way. However, there was a time when Seattle had a thriving jazz scene centered on clubs in the Central District of Seattle that attracted swing bands and such jazz greats as Duke Ellington and Count Basie. Venues like the Black and Tan Club also served as a launching pad for future music legends Quincy Jones (a Seattle native) and Ray Charles (a Seattle transplant for a few years). It was also where talented women, such as Edythe Turnham and the International Sweethearts of Rhythm (the first integrated all-female jazz band), stepped into the male-dominated jazz world and led their own bands.

The music was great, and audiences in the clubs were usually racially integrated. Still, Black musicians were shut out from playing venues outside of the Central District due to segregation and redlining. Well-paying clubs and theaters in areas like downtown were closed to Black musicians, clearly impacting their ability to earn more money.

Black musicians wanted a union to ensure that they were treated fairly in pay and to negotiate fair contracts. The union in Seattle for musicians,

Music sheet. *Public domain.*

the American Federation of Musicians (AFM) Local 76, did not allow Black musicians to join. The Local 76 also had a stronghold on where musicians played.

Jazz music was vibrant and alive with great performers. To keep it that way, the Black musicians decided they needed their own union. The first Black Musicians' Union, the Local 458, was established in 1918. "No one did more to keep jazz alive in Seattle than pianist Gertrude Harvey Wright (who played jazz piano), who helped found the short-lived Black Musicians' Union after World War I," said Eric Bronson, the digital advocacy and engagement manager at the YWCA. "She was an active union organizer there, as well as the Local 493 segregated union that followed," he said.

The Local 458 operated from 1918 to 1923, with musician Paul Barnett as president. The union was effective, as Black musicians were getting jobs outside of the Central District. That enraged the Local 76, which retaliated by filing complaints of minor governance breaches and financial improprieties with the International Union Headquarters, asking for their charter to be revoked, which it did on April 22 the same year. Black musicians were without a union for more than eight months. Local 76 finally relented on its attacks, and on November 22, 1924, a new union, the AFM Local 493, had more than fifty-five members within six months. Paul Barnett was again elected president. Gertrude Harvey and other women musicians, such as Edythe Turnham and Virginia Hughes, joined the union and made it strong. As time went on, women such as pianist and composer Patti Bown, Ernestine Anderson, Evelyn Bundy Taylor, Derniece "Melody" Jones and Ruby Bishop joined as well, according to Historylink.org. The women comprised about 10 percent of the union's membership. "Even though men formally headed the unions, it was the women members who were the backbone of the organization," Bronson said in his article "Black Women Who Save Jazz." "It was the women's organizational skills that made the union." The Local 493 welcomed Asian, Filipino, Latino and even some white musicians into the union as time went on.

The jazz scene in Seattle flourished from the 1920s and only slowed in the 1950s. The union was essential in closing the pay gap between white and Black musicians.

Local 493 union members often congregated at the Blue Note Club located at 1319 Jefferson Street. It was known for hosting legendary jam sessions. On any given night, you could find Ray Charles, Quincy Jones, Patti Bown and a host of great jazz musicians playing the night away. It wasn't unusual for luminaries such as Cab Calloway and Duke Ellington to come to the Blue Note to play.

In 1958, Local 493 and Local 76 put their differences aside and merged in one union, Local 76-493.

22

PATTI BOWN

Internationally Renowned Jazz Pianist, Composer and Singer

Patti Bown was a world-renowned jazz singer, pianist and composer. She was a child prodigy who began playing the piano at two years old. She played with greats such as Quincy Jones and Billy Eckstine and composed for such jazz greats as Sarah Vaughan and Duke Ellington.

The internationally renowned jazz pianist, composer and singer Patti Bown became one of the most sought-after jazz artists at a time when jazz was a man's world. She was a true trailblazer in the music world. She has been described in many ways—she was bold, headstrong, outspoken, adventurous—but there is one thing everyone agrees on: she was extremely talented and unique.

Bown and another Seattle music legend, Quincy Jones, were childhood friends. She played with the greats such as Billy Eckstine, Cal Massey and Gene Ammons. She was also music director and composer for singers like Sarah Vaughn and Dinah Washington.

Patricia Anne Bown was born on July 26, 1931, in Seattle, Washington, to parents Augustas and Edith Bown. Raised in the Central District of Seattle, she was a child prodigy. "I started playing the piano when I was two years old," she said in a PBS interview with Marian McPartland. "I played by ear. I was from a large family, and we had perfect pitch." At three years old, she was playing along with the likes of Duke Ellington, according to music writer Steve Wallace.

Bown started playing the piano when she was two years old. *Public domain.*

Bown grew up in a home filled with classical music and culture. Her mother played the piano, and one of her sisters, Edith Mary, became a classical pianist. Her mother was friends with opera great Marian Anderson, the first Black American to perform at the Metropolitan Opera. "We had grand piano–playing night at our house. That's probably why I wanted to play so much," Bown said in her PBS interview. Her mother insisted that the girls play classical or gospel music, but Bown had other ideas. "When I walked home from school, I passed the pool parlor and the Mardi Gras, and they always had jazz playing. My mother was saying 'No!' but the music was sensual, and it said 'Yes!'" This is still a well-known quote from Bown.

In 1949, Bown received a music scholarship to Seattle University. She later transferred to the University of Washington. Her musical talent was evident, and she played with the Seattle Symphony in 1952.

Even though her parents were against her playing jazz music, they relented, and Bown began playing the local jazz clubs on Jackson Street. At the age of twenty-two, she joined the Black Musicians' Union. Bown joined fellow musicians Quincy Jones, Floyd Standifer and Seattle transplant Ray

Patti Bown playing at the New Orleans Restaurant in Seattle in 1989. *Photograph courtesy of MOHAI, the Seattle Post-Intelligencer Collection.*

Charles for rousing jam sessions at the Blue Note Club on East Jefferson Street (not to be confused with the renowned Blue Note Club in the Village in New York). Bown considered Ray Charles a mentor, and she credits him with teaching her how to accompany singers in a band.

At the age of twenty-four, Bown moved to New York City to fulfill her dream to become a jazz musician.

Bown reconnected with her old friend Quincy Jones, who gave her excellent references. However, it was still hard for Bown to get regular work at first. "I think I was scared when I first started traveling," she said in the PBS interview. "It was a period when it was really hard for women. Men didn't really respect us—like how we got there because we were pretty or cute, not because we had spent time learning the craft. It's so wonderful to be part of this age where there are so many women playing and composing today."

Bown moved to the Village, home to artists at the time, in New York. The Village was home to great jazz clubs like the legendary Blue Note.

Bown adapted quickly to the New York music scene. In an article titled "Patti Bown Overcoming in Triplicate," writer Steven Wallace described her technique as "eclectic, unpredictable—which ran the gamut from Fats Waller through bebop to flirtations."

Bown described her style in the PBS interview, "I like to play odd-metered notes. One of the things about big band playing is learning when not to play—when to feel some kind of rhythmic lick. Most people overplay when they do solos. You have to leave space, accompany them, and make them feel stimulated and get out of their way. Rhythm is very important to me. I think I might have been a dancer in a past life."

In the PBS interview, Bown told McPartland that one of her musical influences was the song "Chelsea Bridge," composed by Billy Strayhorn. His noted composition includes "Take the 'A' Train," "Lush Life" and "Chelsea Bridge." "'Chelsea Bridge' was one of the first records that I listened to over and over. That record had it going on, and those saxophones—what were they doing?" she said.

Her career took off in New York. In 1957, she played with Dinah Washington, described as "the most popular Black female recording artist of the 1950s." Steve Wallace said blues artists loved her. "Artists like Etta Jones, Eddie 'Cleanhead Vinson,' and even R&B soul artists like Aretha Franklin and James Brown, whom she worked with also."

Bown formed a trio and, in 1958, made her first and only album as a leader titled *Patti Bown Plays Big Band* for Columbia Records. The album features her song "G'won Train," which became a crowd favorite. It's unclear why Bown never made another album on her own. However, her discography with Quincy Jones was extensive, so much so that she earned the nickname "the swinging pianist in the Quincy Jones Orchestra." Her discography also reads like a who's who of jazz and blues greats of the 1950s and 1960s. "When I started playing, I had no experience as a big band pianist," she said in her PBS interview. "I learned to be a big band pianist by being one—you listen to yourself and go from there," Wallace said big bands were a perfect setting for Bown. "Her full sound stood out in them, and she had the sensitivity to weave in and out of backgrounds and the power to drive the rhythm sections in larger groups."

In 1959, she joined Quincy Jones, who had been hired as musical director of a European tour production titled *Free and Easy*, a blues opera. They were in Paris, and Jones had assembled an amazing band. However, the show closed after a few weeks due to lackluster ticket sales. Unfortunately, the band was left in the precarious situation of being broke and stuck in Europe. They managed to pick up enough gigs to return home.

In 1997, Bown performed at the Kennedy Center, an event she treasured as a great honor.

On March 21, 2008, Bown died from kidney failure at a nursing facility in Media, Pennsylvania.

Bown was an in-demand pianist and composer. In the 1960s, she recorded extensively with artists such as Duke Ellington, George Russell and Cal Massey and composed music for Sarah Vaughan and Duke Ellington. In the 1970s, she worked in the orchestra pit for Broadway shows and in television shows and films.

Bown made a career as a jazz pianist in a time when women weren't welcomed. Writer Steve Wallace sums up her career this way: "After overcoming her mother's resistance and God knows what else, she came to New York as a twenty-four-year-old, and with her skill and ballsy, creative playing, quickly impressed some of the best, toughest jazzmen who ever lived. At a time when jazz was strictly a men's club, Patti Bown took a seat—not just at the boys' table, but the big boys' table."

23

EDYTHE TURNHAM AND HER KNIGHTS OF SYNCOPATION

Edythe Turnham and her band were popular performers in the Seattle music scene. She began playing the piano when she was only three years old.

Edythe Turnham was a child prodigy who began playing the piano at three years old. She was also one of the women who broke the glass ceiling in the jazz music genre by being a bandleader in her own band and one of the first four women to join the Black Musicians' Union when it formed in Seattle.

She was born Edythe Pane on March 24, 1890, in Topeka, Kansas. Her family moved to Spokane in 1900. She and her sister Maggie loved music and loved performing. When she was ten, she, her father and her sister developed an act and toured with a vaudeville troupe. Vaudeville was popular from the 1900s to the 1930s. A vaudeville troupe consisted of acts ranging from jazz music, comedy and dance to juggling.

When Edythe Pane was a teenager, she met and married Floyd Turnham in 1908. He was a carpenter from Texas. They had two children together.

The couple moved to Seattle. "When band leader Edythe Turnham moved from Spokane to Seattle, her son Floyd started 'dancing for dimes' in front of the Black and Tan Club," said Paul DeBarros and Patrick MacDonald in a *Seattle Times* article titled "Seattle's Fun and Noise."

Turnham assembled a band: Edythe Turnham and Her Knights of Syncopation. Its members included Turnham on piano, Floyd on drums, Floyd Jr. (who joined the band at fifteen) on saxophone and her sister Maggie

Edythe Turnham and her band were popular performers in the Seattle music scene. *Public domain.*

as a dancer and entertainer. They were regulars at Seattle jazz clubs during jazz's heyday in Seattle. The band was one of the best and consistently scored jobs at the clubs.

At one point, the band performed on cruise ships along the West Coast. The Turnhams relocated to Los Angeles and renamed the band the Dixie Aces. They were very successful.

Floyd Turnham died in 1936; reportedly, Edythe continued working until 1945. Floyd Jr. continued to have a successful career as a saxophone player.

Edythe Turnham died in 1950 from complications from diabetes. Turnham was a great musician who earned the respect of other musicians in a world dominated by men.

24

RUBY BISHOP

Seattle Hall of Fame's First Lady of Jazz

Ruby Bishop was a legendary Seattle jazz performer. The U.S. Army recruited her to perform for the troops in South Korea and Vietnam. She also played for audiences in London, Paris and other international locations. Bishop had a long friendship with legendary performer Louis Armstrong.

Ruby Bishop started performing as a dancer when she was a child and continued to perform as a renowned jazz pianist until she was ninety-six years old. "The lady knew how to make an entrance too in the ankle-length, gold-hued raincoat she donned on stormy winter nights," according to an article from the *Seattle Film and Music Blog*. "Then, there's the splendid sequined wardrobe she wears to perform."

Ruby Carol Cogwell was born on December 22, 1919, on a farm in Thurston County in Washington. Bishop was actually the first Black baby born in Thurston County. She was the last of eight children. Ruby loved to perform. As a young child, her brother brought home a piano, and she taught herself to play. "I was in show business when I was six years old," she said in a KIRO radio interview conducted by Rachel Belle in 2012. "I was making a lot of money singing and dancing, especially at county fairs when they would come to town. They would throw money from the grandstands." Bishop was fronting her own twelve-piece band known as the Centralia Buccaneers.

Music was in Bishop's blood, and she was a bright student. When she graduated from high school, her parents insisted that she go to college. She attended the University of Washington. However, Bishop wanted to be a musician, but her mother had other ideas. "[My] mother wouldn't let me take music in college. She wanted me to be a pharmacist. I didn't like any of the sciences," Bishop said. "I wanted to play music, so I took off." After a year of college, she left school. "I never looked back because I didn't want to be a pharmacist. I wasn't sorry for what I did." Ironically, Bishop ended up marrying Alex Bishop, who was a pharmacist.

Bishop worked many jobs on her journey to become a hall of fame musician. During World War II, she worked for Boeing as a mechanic and draftsman as part of the war effort. She also worked as a beautician, a court reporter and even a cabinetmaker while working at night as a musician.

Music was always close to her heart, and in her fifties, she was such an accomplished performer that the U.S. Army recruited her to entertain the troops in South Korea and Vietnam. "It was great going to Vietnam and Korea. I really got a kick out of those guys," Bishop said in the KIRO interview.

During this time, Bishop also became an international performer, appearing in locations such as London, Paris and Stockholm.

Bishop was one of the first performers to join the Black Musicians' Union, Local 498, in the early 1900s. She was a busy musician playing jazz venues around town; she was restricted to playing clubs in the Central District, mainly along Jackson Street, because of redlining and segregation. Jackson Street was the king of live music, and jazz sat atop the throne.

Bishop's time playing the Jackson Street clubs was a wonderful time for her. Her brother was an agent of the Black Musicians' Union (Local 498) and was acquainted with all the famous Black performers who came to Seattle to perform. "He would bring me along when musicians like Cab Calloway, Duke Ellington and Fats Waller—all the greats would come to the Blue Note Club [headquarters to Local 498]," she said in a KCTS9 interview in 2013. Bishop became friends with the greats. She was especially fond of legendary trumpeter and singer Louis Armstrong. "He was just a good guy," she said in the KIRO interview. "He made me happy. He and I were good friends, and when he came to anyone's home, it was mine." Bishop's home became the go-to spot for the luminaries who came to Seattle to perform. It wasn't unusual for major stars like Billy Eckstine, Cab Calloway and, of course, Louis Armstrong to go to Bishop's house wanting a home-cooked meal. Armstrong's entire band would usually show up. "I would ask the guys, 'Hey, would you like for me to fix dinner for you tonight?' Of course, they said yes," she said. Bishop said she would

Ruby Bishop performing at Ivar's Restaurant in Seattle in 1958. *Photograph courtesy of MOHAI, the Seattle Post-Intelligencer Collection. 2000.107.022.17.01.*

spend the day shopping and cooking their favorite meals. "When they got done with work at night, here come the taxi cabs stopping at my house. Oh gosh, we would have more fun." She remained friends with Armstrong, and the two frequently talked over the years until he died in 1971.

In her interview with KCTS9, Bishop credits her style to another great musician, Fats Waller. Waller, a jazz pianist, composer, violinist and singer, was one of the most famous entertainers during his time; "Ain't Misbehaving" is one of his most-well-known compositions. "I got a lot of my inspiration from him," Bishop said. She said her favorite song to play was "Your Feets Too Big."

In her later years, Bishop became somewhat legendary by continuing to play musical lounges in Seattle. She played at Martins, and in 2010, when she was ninety years old, she became a regular piano performer at Vito's restaurant. She was an engaging performer, often mingling with the audience, laughing and talking.

"You can tell that the piano comes as naturally as breathing to her, and she holds a grace and ease that you don't [see] very often," said Craig Lungren, Vito's owner, in an article from the *Capitol Hill Seattle Blog*. "She still has mischief in her eyes and a sharp wit."

In 2016, Gibson was inducted into the Seattle Jazz Hall of Fame at the Golden Ear Awards. Gibson retired that same year, and Vito's threw her a party.

Bishop's first husband died, and she remarried Arthur Schelling in 2002, when she was eighty-two. Ruby Bishop died on June 23, 2019, at ninety-nine years of age.

25

PEGGY JOAN MAXIE

The First Black Woman Elected to Washington State Legislature

Peggy Joan Maxie was the first Black woman elected to the Washington State legislature. She was elected in 1970 and served for six terms. Maxie sponsored the Landlord-Tenant Act.

Peggy Joan Maxie is a pioneering legislator. She became the first Black woman legislator elected in Washington State. In 1970, Maxie was elected to the Washington State House of Representatives. She served six consecutive terms before being defeated in 1982 by the state's future governor Gary Locke.

Maxie's foray into politics was serendipitous. According to Historylink.org, her brother, Fred Maxie, had decided to run for the House of Representatives but instead went to law school. Her brother Bob literally called her from the sign shop where campaign posters with the name "Maxie" had already been printed and convinced his sister to run. Robert Maxie knew his way around politics. He was a longtime member of the Democratic Party and was instrumental in his sister's campaign. He helped with fundraising and even convinced Jim McGill, a professor at the University of Washington, to work as her campaign manager. It was a winning combination, as Maxie was elected to represent the Thirty-Seventh District in Seattle.

Maxie was born on August 18, 1936, in Amarillo, Texas. Her father, Cleveland Maxie, was an auto mechanic, and her mother, Rebecca, was a housewife. During World War II, the Boeing Aircraft Company had a mass recruitment period, and people from all over the country came to Seattle

A poster from Peggy Maxie's election campaign. *Courtesy of the Washington State Historical Society.*

to work. In 1942, after her parents divorced, and her mother moved with her four kids to Seattle in the hopes of working for Boeing. She did get the job.

Maxi was an excellent student while in school. When her family moved to Seattle, she enrolled in the Immaculate Conception School in the first grade and continued until she graduated from high school. She attended Seattle University and received a degree in psychology. It was a busy next couple of years for Maxie. In between her campaigning for public office, she began graduate school at the University of Washington. She received special permission from the dean of social work to campaign and attend school. In 1972, she graduated from the program with a master's degree in social work. Her thesis was on no-fault divorce law. The following year, no-fault divorce was passed by the Washington legislature.

Maxie proved to be a savvy legislator. One of her first acts as a lawmaker was to prevent redistricting plans for the Central District. Maxie filed an affidavit outlining that the Central District had been undercounted for years. A federal court ultimately agreed with Maxie.

Maxie served on several committees during her tenure. She was a member of the Appropriations Committee, considered one of the most powerful committees. The Appropriations Committee oversees the operating budget. She was also a member of the Judicial and Rules Committees. The Rules Committee determines when and in what order bills will reach the floor of the House.

Maxie also sponsored the Landlord-Tenant Act of Washington State in 1973. The bill established tenants' and landlords' rights and responsibilities, such as evictions guidelines, landlords maintaining the property and giving tenants at least forty-eight-hours' notice before entering a dwelling.

Maxi also chaired the House of Higher Education Committee. According to Historylink.org, the governor had asked for an increase in tuition for universities and colleges. Much to the dismay of her Republican colleagues, Maxie held up the bill because she believed that the bill needed to be studied. After all, it affected so many people in the community.

Peggy Joan Maxie was the first Black woman elected to the Washington State Legislature. *Photograph courtesy of the Washington State Archives, Susan Parish Photograph Collection.*

"We need to have time for more citizen input because raising tuition has consequences for all kinds of people, like veterans, working mothers, the poor," she was quoted saying on Historylink.org. She proposed a citizens' task force to study the issues.

Maxie also sponsored a bill that brought the first driver's license testing center to the Central Area.

Maxie cosponsored the Displaced Homemakers Act, a bill that helped women who had been homemakers but later in life, because of divorce or death of a spouse, found themselves facing the prospect of finding jobs. The Displaced Homemakers Act provided training and services through community colleges.

In 1981, Maxie began conducting legislative workshops to explain to the average citizen how the legislature works. The University of Washington acknowledged her for the workshops. She considered it a great honor.

After Locke defeated her in 1982, Maxie returned to civilian life and became a mental health therapist.

Maxie received an honorary doctorate from St. Martin's University in Lacey, Washington.

26

JANE A. RULEY

The First Black Woman Teacher in Washington State

The Sheridan School District hired Jane Ruley on March 27, 1897, making her the first Black teacher in Kitsap County and the first Black teacher in Washington State.

J ane Ruley made history when the Shelton School District in Kitsap
County hired her on March 27, 1897, as a teacher for the Sheridan
School. The hiring made her the first Black woman teacher in Kitsap
County, and historians believe she was the first Black woman hired to teach
in Washington State.

Ruley was born in 1856 in Berkley, Virginia, as Lilly Jane Archer. Details
about her earliest life are not well known. However, records show she was
the daughter of an enslaved person and was always an excellent student.
After graduation from high school, she attended the General Armstrong
School, a teacher training school in Hampton, Virginia, now known as
Hampton Institute. She was the valedictorian of her class. Graduating at
the top of her class was no easy feat, because according to Historylink.org,
Booker T. Washington was one of her classmates. Washington, the famed
educator, author and advisor to several presidents, was essential in founding
the Tuskegee Institute (a historically Black college) in Tuskegee, Alabama.

Ruley graduated from college in 1875. She eventually moved to Kitsap
County in the hopes of becoming a teacher. There, she met and married her
husband, Paul E. Ruley, who would become one of the pioneers of Kitsap
County. Paul Ruley was born in Stuttgart, Germany, in 1852. His parents

Students in Ruley's class. She was hired on March 27, 1897. *Courtesy of the Living Arts Cultural Heritage Project, Kitsap County.*

moved to the United States when he was two years old. The family initially moved to Oneida, New York. He attended school there until he was eleven or twelve years old before deciding to strike out on his own. He moved to the Northwest and landed in Kitsap County. Despite his limited formal education, he and his wife were strong education proponents. Ruley and her husband served on the Sheridan School Board.

According to news reports, the couple was devoted to their community, and the community embraced them. They were prominent citizens of the community.

The Sheridan School was located on the Ruleys' property, near Sheridan Road and Schley Boulevard. Jane Ruley was proud of the school, and she was a devoted teacher.

The Ruleys had two children: a son, Archie, and a daughter, Gertrude. Both went to college; Archie attended Washington College, and Gertrude attended Washington State College in Pullman, Washington. She graduated with honors with a bachelor's degree in music.

Paul Ruley died on September 18, 1913. Jane Ruley died in 1927.

27

MARJORIE E. PITTER KING

The First Black Woman to Serve in the Washington State Legislature

Marjorie Pitter King was the first Black woman to serve in the Washington State legislature. She was appointed in 1965. She was active in Democratic Party politics, attending several national conventions. Pitter King was also a prominent Seattle businesswoman.

Marjorie E. Pitter King was a remarkable trailblazer. On September 2, 1965, she was appointed to serve the unexpired term of Representative Ann O'Donnell, who died before her tenure was up. This appointment made King the first Black woman to serve in the Washington State legislature. King also holds the distinction of being one of the earliest Black businesswomen. She was the owner and operator of M&M Accounting and Tax Service for forty-eight years. "She was a mover and shaker all her life," said Maxine Haynes in her sister's obituary in the *Seattle Times*.

King was born Marjorie Pitter on March 8, 1921, to parents Edward A. Pitter and Marjorie Allen Pitter in Seattle, Washington. Edward Pitter was one of the earliest settlers and pioneers of Washington. He was born in Jamaica in 1892. Pitter moved to Seattle in 1909. He arrived in Seattle during the Alaska-Yukon Pacific Exposition as a captain's steward on a passenger liner, according to Historylink.org. Pitter liked the area and decided to stay. He became a King County clerk. The Pitters set the tone for their children to become involved with politics. Pitter was a member of the Colored Democratic Club of King County. According to Historylink.org, in 1963, he was honored as the Democrat of the Year. Pitter's mother, Marjorie, was one of the founders of the Colored Woman's Progressive Democratic

Club of King County. King was the youngest of the three daughters: Constance, Maxine and Marjorie. Forever the businesswoman, it started when she was young. "When we were kids, Marjorie pressed my sister and me into helping her start a business—Tres Hermanas, or 'Three Sisters.' She bought a mimeograph machine and ran off Christmas cards and sold them."

The Pitters bought a house at Twenty-Fourth Avenue and Pine Street. "When we moved into our house, the neighbors did sign a petition to keep us out," King told Historylink.org. "But it didn't mean anything, and we just ignored it; there were no restrictive covenants."

King was the first Black woman to serve in the Washington State Legislature. *Public domain.*

The Pitters sisters attended Garfield High School. The three were also accepted to the University of Washington, where Majorie majored in accounting. Unlike her sisters, Majorie struggled. She said she endured racial epithets and was placed on academic probation because of her low grades. King admitted that she felt out of place at the university. She transferred to Howard University in Washington, D.C., to complete her degree. Howard University is one of the nation's preeminent HBCUs (historically Black colleges and universities). Before she could graduate, another opportunity presented itself to King. She left school in 1942 to work for the Pentagon during World War II.

Pitter returned to Seattle in 1944. She married John T. King, and they had two sons, Walton and Edward.

In 1944, King started her tax business. "She had clients from Mexico, Alaska, all over," said her sister in the *Seattle Times* obituary. "She would do them for people who could not read or write English and even wrote letters for them." King successfully operated her business until she sold the company in 1995.

King always had an interest in politics, according to her nephew Kenneth Thomas. "I found a letter dated 1946 from Eleanor Roosevelt, thanking her for organizing a group of young Democrats."

King was the Thirty-Seventh District Party chair, vice-chair on the rules, credentials, platform committee and the Metropolitan Democratic Women Inc. She attended the 1964 and 1968 National Democratic Conventions. At the 1968 convention in Chicago, she was tear-gassed when riots broke out.

On September 2, 1965, King was appointed to complete the term of Ann O'Donnell representing the Thirty-Seventh District, making her the first Black woman to serve in the Washington State legislature and the first Black woman to be appointed to the legislature. She ran for the position in 1966 but lost.

King served as chairwoman of the Thirty-Seventh District for the Democratic Party and treasurer for the Washington State Federation of Democratic Women.

King was also an active community member. She was on the board of the YWCA and a member of the Washington State Women's Civil Rights Committee. King was a board member of the Urban League, a proponent of civil rights for women and minorities. King was also a member of the Delta Sigma Theta sorority and a member of the Black Heritage Society of Washington State.

Majorie Pitter King died on January 28, 1996. "She was a little bulldog," said Thomas in her obituary. "She got it from her father."

28

FRANCES L. SCOTT

The First Black Woman to Become a Lawyer in Spokane

Frances Scott was a beloved teacher and community leader who became the first Black woman attorney in Spokane. After becoming an attorney, she continued to teach during the day and practiced law in the evenings.

Frances L. Scott is an iconic figure in Spokane. She was not only a beloved teacher and community leader, but she also holds the distinction of being the first Black woman attorney in Spokane.

Scott was born on November 4, 1921. She was the great-granddaughter of freed people. Her mother, Marie Maley, a single mother of four, moved the family to Spokane when Scott was a baby. Her mother worked as a nurse at Grady Memorial Hospital in Atlanta. However, as reported in the *Spokesman-Review*, Spokane hospitals didn't hire Black nurses. Maley had to make a living, so to support her family, she went to work as a cook at a brothel, making twelve dollars a week.

Scott graduated from Mary Cliff High School with excellent grades.

While in high school, Scott experienced racism on a personal level. She often told the story of her hoped-for encounter with the world-renowned opera singer Marian Anderson. She and two of her white classmates wanted to interview Anderson for the school newspaper. The Davenport hotel staff refused to let Scott ride the elevator and directed her to the freight elevators when they got there. "My white friends—bless their hearts, decided if I had to ride the freight elevator, they would too," said Scott. "But when we finally got upstairs, we couldn't find Marian Anderson. As it turned out, she hadn't

Scott was a member of the school's glee club in 1944. *Photograph courtesy of the Whitworth University Archives and Special Collections.*

been allowed to stay in the Davenport Hotel because she was Black. We finally found her around the corner at the little Pemberton Hotel."

While attending Holy Names College, Scott married Vernon Scott, a divorced chiropractor; she left school before graduating. "The good nuns put her out because she married a divorced man in her senior year," said her sister Ruth Nichols in a *Spokesman-Review* article. Scott, however, continued her education and attended Whitworth College in Spokane, receiving both a bachelor's degree and a master's degree. She received her teaching certificate from Whitworth as well. In the Whitworth College archives, Scott said, "Whitworth gave this Black woman an opportunity when it was far from commonplace. They gave it, I took it and I'm glad I did."

Scott began her teaching career at Rogers High School in 1958; there, she taught English, German, sociology and Black history. Scott also reached out to other students who needed academic support by teaching part time at Fort Wright College Upward Bound Program. The Upward Bound Program, in some instances, serves students from low-income families or students who need academic support. Scott was compassionate when it came to students and ensuring their ability to learn.

Scott was one of only four Black teachers when she started teaching. She was well aware of the importance of her role as a teacher and what it represented to both Black and white students. "They need to see Black people in some roles other than scrubbing floors," she said in the *Spokesman-Review* article.

Scott was also a strong supporter of civil rights and worked hard to strengthen equality. She had seen her share of inequality. She recounted that as a child, dentists in Spokane would often only work on Black patients after hours so that the appearances of Black people wouldn't scare away their other clientele, according to *Spokesman-Review.*

Scott was a lifetime member of the NAACP and looked for other ways to help people. She made a significant decision about her life and decided to go to law school. In 1974, she was accepted to Gonzaga University of Law and graduated in 1978. After passing the Bar, she became the first Black woman in Spokane to practice law. Despite her new role as a lawyer, Scott continued to teach at Rogers High School during the day. She was committed to helping the poor and minority communities navigate the legal system. So, Scott worked at night for the community pro bono. When she graduated, she said, "I want to be able to instruct, as well as represent minority people in their dealing with the law."

Scott was known for her sense of humor, as demonstrated when she returned to Whitworth to accept her Distinguished Alumna Award in 2005. "People who live in glass houses are apt to be fascinating, and no matter what the problem is, chocolate is the answer." At the same event, she said, "We are in this together, and that's what makes it bearable."

Scott's husband and mother died in 1988. Shortly after, she moved to Port Orchard, Washington, to open bed-and-breakfast with one of her friends.

Scott graduated from Whitworth University. She was in the choir and the glee club. *Courtesy of Whitworth University Archives and Special Collections.*

Frances Scott was a beloved teacher and attorney in Spokane. *Photograph courtesy of the Spokane Public Schools' archives.*

Scott was the keynote speaker at Dr. Martin Luther King Jr.'s remembrance at Spokane Community College in 2000, where she said, "We have made progress, but we have not reached the end of the journey. Dr. King's dream is not a reality yet. But as long as we are moving in the direction of the dream, we will succeed."

Sheridan Elementary School was renamed Frances Scott Elementary. *Courtesy of Spokane Public Schools.*

Frances Scott was a champion of education. In 2001, she received another honor when the City of Spokane renamed Sheridan Elementary School Frances L. N. Scott Elementary School.

"Having the opportunity to name a school after anybody is a tremendous honor, but having an opportunity to name a school after a Black woman who has the resume and has given their entire life to making a better community in a better world as Scott did was an honor of a lifetime," said Jerrall Haynes, Spokane's civil officer and past president of the school board, to Converge Media.

"As someone who's from the community, as a Black woman, it is an honor just to know that her name was considered. It's a win, and to know that I went to that school, it makes me feel good," said Lisa Gardner, director of communications for Spokane City Council, who also spoke to Converge Media.

Haynes continued saying in the interview that Scott dedicated her life to service. "In her 30 years teaching and serving students every single day and getting her law degree, and doing pro bono Civil Rights law work for cases for people in the evenings. It was absolutely unbelievable that there were people out there during those years that were willing to lay it all on the line, and Frances just took that charge and ran with it."

Scott was a member of and headed many organizations:

- In 1977, she was a delegate to the National Women's Conference in Spokane.
- In 1979, she was appointed to the Civil Service Commission, becoming the first Black person and the first woman commissioner in history.
- In the early 1980s, Scott served two terms as president of the Spokane Education Association.
- In 1985, Governor Booth Gardner appointed Scott to a seven-year term on the Washington State University board of regents, and she served one year as president.
- According to her obituary, Scott and her husband had three daughters. She was preceded in death by one of her daughters.

DR. MAXINE MIMMS

The First Black Woman to Establish a College

Dr. Maxine Mimms is an activist, educator and founder of the Evergreen State College in Tacoma. She taught elementary school in Seattle. She has a long line of education accolades. Before Evergreen State College came to fruition, Mimms began teaching adult students out of her home because she wanted to make education available to everyone.

D r. Maxine Mimms has devoted her life to educating. She is an activist, educator and founder of the Evergreen State College in Tacoma.

Mimms has become an education expert over the years. The influential educator has consulted with and offered her expertise to global education institutions, including Oprah Winfrey's Leadership Academy for Girls in South Africa.

On March 4, 1928, Mimms was born in Newport News, Virginia. Her parents, Benson and Isabella Buie, were staunch supporters of education and political activism passions they passed down to their five children. Her mother was determined to teach anyone willing to learn. She taught their neighbors to read at their dining room table, according to "Her Story," written by Lori Larson for the Legacy Washington Project for the office of the secretary of state. Her father was a supporter of civil rights activist and orator Marcus Garvey. "The story in my house was improvement," said Mimms.

The family lived close to Hampton University, a HBCU in Hampton, Virginia. They often went to the college to hear prominent Black Americans and civil rights activists of that era speak on issues affecting Black Americans.

Left: Dr. Mimms at Colman Elementary Seattle Public Schools in 1962 or 1963. *Photograph courtesy of Seattle Public Schools, Colman-Thurgood Marshall Collection.*

Right: Dr. Mimms was one of the first Black Americans promoted to an administrative position for the Seattle Public School System. *Courtesy of the* Legacy Washington *exhibit.*

Mimms graduated with honors from Huntington High School in 1952. "When I was growing up, college was not an option in my home," Mimms said. Following graduation, she attended Virginia Union University (a HBCU), earning her bachelor's degree. According to Mimms, attending Virginia Union was an exciting time in her life. She explained that she got the opportunity to know future civil rights leaders Dr. Samuel McKinney and Dr. Martin Luther King Jr., who were roommates at Morehouse College in Atlanta, Georgia. "Morehouse students would often come to Vesper services at Virginia Union," she said in the Legacy Project story.

She subsequently earned her master's degree from Wayne State University in Detroit, Michigan, where she met her husband, Jack Mimms. She went on to earn a doctorate in education administration from Union Graduate College.

"It was mandatory in our neighborhood to go to college," Mimms said in the Legacy Project story. "In the midst of segregation, Black teachers spotted the brightest kids and gave them marching orders....The teachers would say, we are going to need doctors [and other professionals]."

In 1953, Mimms moved to Seattle after her husband took a job with the Boeing Company. Mimms began teaching. One school she taught at was Leschi Elementary School, where one of Seattle's favorite sons, Jimi Hendrix, attended school.

In 1964, Mimms was one of a few Black individuals promoted to an administrative position for the Seattle Public Schools. The Legacy Project stated that it was such an unusual event that it made headlines in the *Seattle Times*. The headline read, "4 Negroes Named as Administrators."

Mimms's career continued to expand. In 1968, she became project director for a teacher in-service sensitivity training program. The year 1968 was a pivitol one in the United States with the assassinations of Martin Luther King Jr. and Robert Kennedy. It was also a pivotal year in Seattle. There was a battle between the school district and civil rights organizations surrounding the segregation of Seattle schools. Historic housing redlining had divided the city along racial lines. Most Black people lived in areas like the Central District, which forced segregation on a grand scale. The in-service training program was designed to train school employees to understand, accept and make racial minorities feel welcomed in schools. The integration of the Seattle Public Schools would take a long, arduous road to find a solution, experimenting with magnet schools and mandatory busing along the way.

Mimms's career took a different turn in 1969, when the assistant secretary of the U.S. Department of Labor asked Mimms to join him in Washington, D.C., to help implement President Nixon's policy of promoting affirmative action on federal contracts. Mimms worked as a special assistant to Elizabeth Koontz, the Labor Women's Bureau's director. Koontz was the first Black woman to head a department and the highest-ranking woman in the Nixon administration. During her tenure, Koontz established the Human and Civil Rights Division. "She was a powerful and creative woman," Mimms described her in the Legacy Project story. In the 1970s, the women's bureau secured a women's rights victory when the inequality in sports was addressed. The bureau played a role in Title IX in women's sports. Title IX protects people from discrimination based on sex in sports programs receiving federal funds or assistance.

In 1972, Mimms returned to the Pacific Northwest and education by becoming a faculty member of the Evergreen State College in Olympia. "If we could just understand we are all different, but we are all geniuses. The need to recognize that within our own community, there are people who think like Plato, paint like Picasso and meditate like Buddha," she said in the

Legacy Project story. Mimms commuted from Tacoma to Olympia. There was something that kept nagging at her. In her opinion, there was a dearth of affordable higher education institutions in Tacoma. She explained there were two private colleges but no public colleges—other than community colleges. "Every bone in me wanted a reset," she said in the Legacy Project story. "My soul was crying and sad because I was not able to work with people whose skin color looked like mine." In the Legacy Project story, Mimms recalled that while having lunch in Tacoma, she heard two women talking about never having the opportunity to return to school because they worked and had children. "These women said there was no one in Tacoma in the four-year education system who would help people like them."

That realization weighed heavily on Dr. Mimms. However, being a proactive person, she started a process that would change lives. Dr. Mimms and a friend of hers, Betsy Diffendel, began teaching classes for people in Tacoma at her home in the mornings before she commuted to work in Olympia. "Just stop to think about that. Dr. Mimms actually began Evergreen State College in Tacoma at her kitchen table," said Vargas.

Mimms wanted an institution that was convenient for the low-income residents of the Hilltop area in Tacoma. She thought the community deserved more. While working in Olympia, Mimms concentrated on developing an education program to serve working adults. She envisioned a college that focused on the needs of Black adult learners—that's the foundation on which she wanted to develop a new college. Meanwhile, she served students as best she could until there was another solution.

In 1982, that dream was realized when the Evergreen State College Tacoma was officially established. Mimms became the first Black woman in the state of Washington to found a four-year college. The motto of the school is "Enter to Learn, Depart to Serve."

Dr. Mimms is the founder of Evergreen State College in Tacoma. *Photograph courtesy of Legacy Washington Exhibit.*

Dr. Mimms pictured with Chassity Holliman-Douglas at a Juneteenth celebration. *Photograph courtesy of Legacy Washington Exhibit.*

According to the Legacy Project story, there is a framed portrait of Dr. Mimms that can be seen as you walk into the building. It is a tribute to the woman who has spent her career dedicated to helping to educate people in marginalized communities. In 1983, Evergreen State College had 150 graduates with bachelor's degrees, with Black students making up a majority of the students. Mimms said the average age of the students was around thirty. The students came from all walks of life. Mimms said in the Legacy Project story that most of the students were working adults, but she discouraged going to school part time. "I don't like part time," said Mimms. "I don't encourage it. I am from the generation where I like to stretch myself—stretch cognitively and physically. When we reduce our philosophy to part time, we produce a bunch of lazy people."

The events of 1968 changed the way Mimms looked at life. "The murdering of Martin Luther King Jr. and the Kennedys was very painful," she said in the Legacy Project story. "But you have to reimagine what does that mean in terms of you." Vargas said the events led Mimms to reimagining what it means to lead. "We're all interconnected. She comes from a restorative place. We have a living library in Kitsap County because Dr. Mimms broke down barriers and redefined true community. A true community is where everyone has a seat at the table," said Vargas. "That's the type of thinking Dr. Mimms wanted to instill at Evergreen State College."

Dr. Mimms was born in Newport News, Virginia, on March 4, 1928. She came to Seattle in 1953. *Photograph courtesy of Evergreen State College.*

Dr. Mimms retired as the school's executive director at the age of ninety. She was ninety-five years old at the time of this writing, and she said in a recent interview that she had no intention of slowing down. When asked what she thought her legacy would be, she was reluctant to say. She's very humble, so she said perhaps that would be the legacy. "My humility—my willingness to be humble enough to give and to receive." Karen Vargas said Mimms's legacy would be everything she has built. "Her legacy will be a living library—not only the college but everything she's built, her mentoring, her educating, her devotion, everything that she's had a hand in developing, and her insistence on respecting and celebrating each other's culture. We're working with Evergreen to further that legacy."

At ninety-five, she still has an active speaking schedule. "I usually speak on the genius of Black people and reimagining yourself," she said.

Dr. Mimms has lived a full life and believes that life can be whatever you can imagine it to be. But there was an event she could never have imagined in her lifetime—the election of the country's first Black president, Barack Obama. "It was unbelievable and pure joy. I never thought I would see it, and now we have Kamala Harris as vice president. It is something to behold."

Always the consummate teacher, Mimms has formed the Maxine Mimms Academy, a classroom for expelled students from the Tacoma schools. The academy works with students, helping with their schoolwork, mentoring, teaching them how to channel their anger into a positive outlet and finding a pathway back to school. The academy also offers job training.

Mimms's advice for teachers is to get students to interact with one another: "Have joy in design to make people continue with hope," she said in the Legacy Project story.

BIBLIOGRAPHY

Books

De Barros, Paul. *Jackson Street After Dark*. Seattle, WA: Sasquatch Books, 1993.

Hayes, Ralph (contributor). *Northwest Black Pioneers*. N.p.: Bon Marchel, 1988.

Hayes, Ralph. *Tacoma Northwest Black Pioneers: A Centennial Tribute*. N.p.: Bon Marchel, 1994.

Hill, Pauline. *Too Young to Be Old: The Story of Bertha Pitts Campbell*. Seattle, WA: Peanut Butter Publishing, 1981.

Hobbs, Richard S. *The Cayton Legacy: An African American Family*. Seattle: Washington State University Press, 2002.

Mumford, Esther Hall. *Seattle's Black Victorians: 1852–1901*. Toronto, ON: Anansi Press, 1980.

Nimura, Tamiko. *Rosa Franklin: A Life in Health Care, Public Service, and Social Justice*. Olympia: Washington State Legislature Oral History Program, 2020.

Singler, Joan, Jean C. Durning, Bettylou Valentine and Martha "Maid" J. Adams. *Seattle in Black and White*. Seattle: University of Washington Press, 2011.

Taylor, Quintard. *African American Women Confront the West*. Norman: University of Oklahoma Press, 2003.

———. *The Forging of a Black Community: Seattle's Central District from 1870 Through the Civil Rights Era*. Seattle: University of Washington Press, 1994.

UWB Zine Queenz. *Badass Womxn in the Pacific Northwest*. Bothell: University of Washington Bothell and University of Washington Libraries, 2019.

Personal Interviews

Bronson, Eric (digital advocate and engagement manager, YWCA/Seattle/King/Snohomish). Interview with the author, Marilyn Morgan.

Brooks, Fabienne "Fae" (retired chief of Criminal Investigations Division, King County Sheriff's Office). Interview with the author, Marilyn Morgan.

Labovitch, Lisa (Everett Public Library historian). Interview with the author, Marilyn Morgan.

Mimms, Dr. Maxine. Interview with the author, Marilyn Morgan.

Tucker, Cynthia (historian for the Washington State Association of Colored Women's Clubs, Tacoma Chapter). Interview with the author, Marilyn Morgan.

Radio Interviews

Interview of Ruby Bishop. KCTS9. May 13, 2013. https//:www.kcts9.org/.

Marian McPartland hosts Patti Bown. *Piano Jazz*, NPR. July 28, 2017. https//www.npr.org/2017/07/28/539974678.

Rachel Belle's interview of Ruby Bishop. KIRO Radio. March 28, 2012.

Videos

Abebe, Dagmawi. *The Ball Method*. N.p.: May 18, 2020. Amazon Prime Video. https://www.amazon.video.com/miracle-Ball-Method.

"Frances L. Scott Was a Trailblazing Educator and Spokane's First Black Woman Lawyer." Seattle, WA: Converge Media, November 4, 2021.

"Tacoma Park Officially Renamed to Honor First Black Woman to Serve as Washington State Senator." Seattle WA: King 5 News, July 9, 2021.

"Tacoma Park Renamed to Honor First Black Woman to Serve as Washington State Senator." Seattle WA: King 5 News, February 24, 2021.

Other Sources

All Music. "Edythe Turnham." https://www.allmusic.com/artist/edythe-turnham-mn0001010043.

Ballotpedia. "Peggy Joan Maxie." https://www.ballotpedia.org./Peggy-Maxie/.
———. "Rosa Franklin." https://ballotpedia.org/Rosa-Franklin.

Beers, C. "Marjorie Pitter King, Pioneer in Business, State Legislature." *Seattle Times*, February 2, 1996. https://archiveseattletimes.com/archive/19960202/231197.

Botts, G. "PLU Alumna First Black Woman to Serve as State Senator, Dedicated 20 Years in Politics to Health Care, Social Justice." Pacific Lutheran University. May 2, 2016. https://www.plu.edu/news/archive/2016/05/02/rosafranklin/.

Brewster, C. "Alice Ball: How the Woman Who Found a Leprosy Treatment Was Almost Lost to History." *National Geographic*, February 21, 2020. https://www.nationalgeographic.com/science/article.

Brodeur, N. "Ruby Bishop, Seattle Jazz Artist and Queen of the Keys at Vito's Dies at 99." *Seattle Times*, June 27, 2019, https://www.seattletimes.com/seattle-news/.

Brown, A. "Letitia A. Graves (1863–1952)." BlackPast.org. May 9, 2009. https://www.blackpast.org/african-american-history/graves-letitia.

Brown, J. "CORE and the Fight Against Employer Discrimination in 1960s Seattle." Seattle Civil Rights and Labor History Project. https://depts.washington.edu/civilr/core-employer-dis-in-1960s-seattle.

Bruestle, S. "Descendants of Black Snohomish County Citizens." Uncover History. Herald.Net.com. February 13, 2017. https://www.heraldnet.com/life.ancestor-of-black-snohomish-citizens.

Burroughs, Nannie Helen. "Twelve Things the Negro Must Do for Himself." www.nburroughsinfo.or/files/47096873.pdf.

Cobbins-Modica, Q. "Dorothy Hollingsworth (1920–)." BlackPast.org. November 6, 2007. https://www.blackpast.org/african-american-history/hollinsworth-dorothy-1920/.

Cohen, B. "First Hill Club Fixture Ruby Bishop Inducted into Seattle Jazz Hall of Fame." *Capitol Hill Seattle Blog*. March 19, 2016. https://www.capitolhillseattle.com/2016/03/first-hill-club-fixture-ruby-bishop.

Converge Media. "Frances L. Scott Was a Trailblazing Educator and Spokane's First Black Woman Lawyer." November 4, 2021. https://www.whereweconverge.com/post.frances-l-scott.

De Barros, P. "Patti Bown, 76, Lit Up Seattle's Early Jazz Scene." *Seattle Times*, March 18, 2008. https://www.seattletimes.com/entertainment/pattibown.

Demay, D. "20 Powerful Washington Women." *Seattle Post-Intelligencer*, March 11, 2016. https://www.seattlepi.com/local.seattle-history/.

Diaz, E. "Susie Revels Cayton (1870–1943)." BlackPast.org. January 22, 2007. https//www.blackpast.org.african-american-history/race.gender-jazz-local-493-black-women-musicians-seattle-1920-1955/.

Eric, Bronson. "The Black Women Who Saved Seattle Jazz." YWCA/Seattle/King/Snohomish. November 6, 2018. https//www.ywcaworks.org/blogs/firesteel/theblackwomenwhosavedseattlejazz.

Everett Public Library Staff. "Who Was Madame Luella Boyer, a Pioneering African American?" HeraldNet. February 26, 2018. https://www.heraldnet.com/life/who-was-madame-luella-boyer.

Fairbanks, K. "Victoria Freeman's Family Plans Celebration at Longview Park." *Daily News*, August 13, 2018. https://www.tdn.com/news/local/victoria/freeman/.

FBI Newsletter. "Extraordinary Member Profile Article, Fabienne 'Fae' Brooks." March 2009.

Fletcher, P. "Peggy Joan Maxie (1936–)." BlackPast.org. February 2, 2009. https://www.blackpast.org/african-american-history/maxie-peggy-joan-1936.

———. "Rosa Franklin (1927–)." BlackPast.org. December 6, 2008. https://www.blackpast.org/african-american-history-franklin-rosa-1927.

Foley, D. "Patti Bown, Singer, and Pianist: The Long Form Interview." Last Bohemians Project. May 11, 2016. https://lastbohemians,blogspot.com/2016/05/pattibown,singerandpianist.

Goshorn, M. "Susie Revels Cayton 'The Part She Played.'" Seattle Civil Rights and Labor History Project. December 9, 2006. https://www.depts.washington.edu/civilr.susie-cayton-1870-1943.

Hanson, M. "Ruby Bishop (1919–2019)." BlackPast.org. July 10, 2014. https://www.blackpast.org/african-american-history/bishop-ruby-1919-1990/.

Henry, M. "Adams Nora B. (1928–2004)." HistoryLink.org. February 27, 2008. https://www.historylink.org/File/8506.

———. "Bertha Pitts Campbell (1889–1990)." BlackPast.org. January 18, 2007. https:www.blackpast.org/african-american-history/campbell-bertha-pitts-1889-1990.

———. "Campbell, Bertha Pitts (1889–1990)." HistoryLink. October 13, 1998. https://historylink.org/file.28.

———. "Congress of Racial Equality (CORE), Seattle Chapter." HistoryLink.org. September 2, 2011. www.historylink.org.file/9879.

———. "Hollingsworth, Dorothy (b. 1920)." HistoryLink.org. October 24, 1998. www.historylink.org/essay291.

———. "King, Marjorie Pitter (1921–1996)." HistoryLink.org. November 2, 2008. https://www.historylink.org./file/8828.

———. "Kitsap County School District Hires Jane A. Ruley, First African American Teacher in County, on March 27, 1897." HistoryLink. May 10, 2003. https://www.historylink.org./File/5452.

———. "Maxie Peggy (1936–)." HistoryLink. January 8, 2009. https://www.historylink.org/File/8882/.

———. "Nettie Craig Asberry (1865–1968)." HistoryLink. June 3, 2008. https://www.historylink.org/File/8632.

Hughes, J. "Lillian Walker, Civil Rights Pioneer." Washington Legacy Project. 2009. https://www.soswa.gov/legacy/stories.lillian-walker.

Jackson, M. "Alice Augusta Ball (1892–1916)." BlackPast.com. September 20, 2007. https://www.blackpast.org/african-american-history/people-african-american-history/ball-alice-augusta-1892-1916/.

Johnson, J. "Nannie Helen Burroughs: Advocate for Self-Sufficient Black Women." ThoughtCo. January 30, 2021. www.thoughtco./thoughtco.com/nannie-helen-burroughs-biography-3528274.

Jones, J. "Nettie Craig Asberry: Civil Rights Leader, Educator, and Social Worker." BlackThen. May 1, 2020. https://blackthen.com/nettie-craig-asberry-civilrights-leader-and-socialworker.

Kath, L. "A Herfragissuf Nettie Craig Asberry." Washington State Historical Society. www.washingtonhistory.org/wp/.

Kawaida, E. "Maxine Mimms (1928–)." BlackPast.org. May 26, 2019. https://www.blackpast.org/african-american-history/people-african-american-history/maxine-mimms-1928/.

Keller, D. "Race, Gender, Jazz and Local 493: Black Women Musicians in Seattle: 1920–1955." BlackPast.org. July 6, 2010. https//www.blackpast.org/african-american-history/race-gender-jazz-local-493-black-women-musicians-seattle-1920-1955.

Kelly, L. "Chronicling an 'Uneasy Road' to Equality." *Kitsap Daily News*, February 1, 2013. https://www.kitsapdailynews.com/news/chroniciling/.

Kershner, J. "Distinguished Woman Left Us a Legacy." *Spokesman-Review*, October 23, 2010. https://www.spokesman.com/stories.2010/oct/23.

Kershner, K. "Walker, Lillian (1913–2012)." HistoryLink. August 29, 2011. https://.www.historylink.org./File/9912.

Labovitch, L. "Jennie Samuels, President of the State Federation of Colored Women's Clubs Welcomes the Eighth Federation Convention to Everett." HistoryLink.com. October 18, 2018. https://www.historylink.org.

———. "Samuels, Jennie (1868–1948)." HistoryLink. June 30, 2021. https://www.historylink.org.File/21261.

Lange, A., PhD. "National Association of Colored Women's Clubs." Washington State Historical Society. www.washingtonhistory.org.

Legacy Washington. "My Life Is Education." 2018. https://www.sos.wa.gov/-assets/legacy/sixty-eight/maxine-mimms-profile-pdf.

Lowe, T. "Washington State Federation of Colored Women (1917–)." BlackPast.org. February 12, 2007. https://blackpast.org/african-american-history/washington-state-federation-colored-women-1917.

Mason, G. "School Name Finalist: Frances Scott, Spokane's First Black Female Attorney, Championed Education, and Civil Rights." *Spokane-Review*, May 25, 2021. https://www.spokanereview.com/stories/2021/may/25.

Mulder, P. "Nettie. J. Craig Asberry (1865–1968)." BlackPast.org. June 13, 2021. https://www.blackpast.org/african-american-history/people-african-american-history/nettie-j-craig-asberry-1865-1988.

National Association of Colored Women's Clubs. https://wacwc.com/.

Northern, M. "Alice Ball Biography." *Biography*. A&E. March 1, 2018. https://www.biography.com/scientist/alice-ball.

O'Connor, A. "Edythe Turnham Orchestra." BlackPast.org. November 21, 2007. https://www.blackpast.org/african-american-history.edythe-turnham-orchestra.

Royster, J. "Marjorie Edwina Pitter King (1921–1996)." BlackPast.org. February 12, 2007. https://www.blackpast.org/african-american-history/king-marjorie-edwina-pitter-1921-1996.

Scott, G. "Black History Month: Alice Augusta Ball." Researcher's Gateway. February 3, 2020. https://researchersgateway.com.

Seattle King County NAACP. "Unsung Heroes: Fabienne 'Fae' Brooks." February 24, 2020. https://www.seattlekingcountynaacp.org.

Seattle Public Schools. "Seattle Public Schools Scholarship Fund." https://seattleschools.org/departments/seattle-schools-scholarship-fund.

Seattle Times. "Nora B. Adams, Obituary." April 25, 2004. https://www.legacy.com/us/obituaries/seattletimes.

Spokesman-Review. "Francis Scott, Obituary." November 7, 2010. https://www.legacy.com/us/obituaries/spokesman/name/frances-scott-obituary.

Summitt, M. "Luella Boyer: Everett's Pioneer African American Business Woman." Snohomish County Women's Legacy Project. March 20, 2020. https://snohomishwomenslegacy.org/2020/03/20/madame-luella-boyer.

Tacoma History. "Asberry V. Wilson." September 25, 2020. https://tacomahistory.live/2020/09/25/asberry-v-wilson.

Trent, S. "The Black Sorority that Faced Racism in the Suffrage Movement but Refused to Walk Away." *Washington Post*, April 8, 2020. https://www.washingtonpost.com.

Wallace, S. "Patti Bown: Overcoming in Triplicate." May 28, 2017. https://wallacebass.com/pattibown.overcoming-in-triplicate.

Where We Converge. "Manima Wilson: First Black Woman to Graduate From Everett High School." January 14, https://www.wereweconverge.com/post/manima-wilson.

Whitworth University. "Whitworth College Distinguished Alumnae Award: Frances Scott, 2005." January 16, 2015.

Wilson, J. "Patti Bown on Piano." *New York Times*, July 1, 1985. https://www.nytimes.com/1985/07/01/arts/patti-bown-on-piano.

Women in the Legislature. "Peggy Joan Maxie." web.leg.wa.gov/womeninthelegislature/members.maxiep.

———. "Rosa Franklin: Women in the Legislature." web.leg.wa.gov/womeninthelegislature/members.franklinr.

YWCA/Seattle/King/Snohomish. "7 History Making Women of Color from Seattle and the Central District." *Seattle Times*, December 12, 2019. https://www.seattletimes.com/sponsored/7-history.

Oral Histories

Gregory, James, and Trevor Griffey. Interviews of Jean Maid Adams, Joan Singler and Bettylou Valentine (members of CORE). Seattle Civil Rights and Labor History Project. October 6, 2006. https://www.depts.washington.edu/civilr/labor-history.

Griffey, Trevor. "Dorothy Hollingsworth." Seattle Civil Rights and Labor History Project. March 2005. Https://www.depts.washington.edu/civilr.labor-history.

Hughes, John. "Lillian Walker." Washington Oral History Legacy Project. 2009. https://www.sos.wa.gov/legacy/stories/lillian-walker.

Mumford, Esther. "Bertha Pitts Campbell." Washington Oral History Legacy Project. April 23, 1975. https://www.sos.wa.gov./legacy/stories/bertha-pitts-campbell.

———. "Thelma Dewitty." Washington Oral History Legacy Project. https://www.sos.wa.gov/legacy/stories/thelma-dewitty/.

———. "Willetta Riddle Gayton." Washington Oral History Legacy Project. https://www.sos.wa.gov/legacy/stories/willetta-riddle-gayton/.

Tacoma Historical Society. Jessie Koon's interview of Dolores Silas. July 28, 2021.

Warmflash, Anita. "Katherine D. Thompkins." MOHAI Museum, Rosie the Riveter Series. September 1, 2005.

———. "Katie R. Burks." MOHAI Museum, Rosie the Riveter Series. July 28, 2005.

———. "Vivian Layne." MOHAI Museum, Rosie the Riveter Series. September 13, 2005.

Washington Association of Colored Women's Clubs. Historian Cynthia Tucker's interview of Ruby West on Mrs. Victoria Freeman. April 8, 2009.

ABOUT THE AUTHOR

Marilyn Morgan is an author, historian and photographer living in Seattle, Washington. Her published books include *Careen in Criminology* and *Seattle Historic Houses of Worship*, and she contributed to the book *New York Past to Present Photo Tour.*

Marilyn earned a bachelors' degree from Virginia State University and obtained a documentary production certificate from the University of Washington.

She has worked for various media outlets, including writing for a Fortune 500 company.

When she is not writing, she loves traveling and photographing the world, jogging, eating at great restaurants, going to Broadway shows and watching movies and old television shows, particularly Westerns.